EDUCATIONAL TECHNOLOGY IN ACTION

Problem-Based Exercises for Technology Integration

M. D. Roblyer
University of Maryland University College

PEARSON

Merrill
Prentice Hall

Upper Saddle River, New Jersey
Columbus, Ohio

DEDICATION

For Bill and Paige –
The high-touch part of my high-tech life

Vice President and Executive Publisher: Jeffery W. Johnston
Editor: Debra A. Stollenwerk
Development Editor: Kimberly J. Lundy
Editorial Assistant: Mary Morrill
Production Editor: JoEllen Gohr
Production Manager: Pamela D. Bennett
Design Coordinator: Diane C. Lorenzo
Cover Designer: Ali Mohrman
Director of Marketing: Ann Castel Davis
Marketing Manager: Darcy Betts Prybella
Marketing Services Manager: Tyra Poole

NOTE: Every effort has been made to provide accurate and current Internet information in this book. However, the Internet and information posted on it are constantly changing; it is inevitable that some of the Internet addresses listed in this textbook will change.

Pearson Prentice Hall™ is a trademark of Pearson Education, Inc.
Pearson® is a registered trademark of Pearson plc
Prentice Hall® is a registered trademark of Pearson Education, Inc.
Merrill® is a registered trademark of Pearson Education, Inc.

Pearson Education Ltd.
Pearson Education Singapore Pte. Ltd.
Pearson Education Canada, Ltd.
Pearson Education—Japan

Pearson Education Australia Pty. Limited
Pearson Education North Asia Ltd.
Pearson Educación de Mexico, S.A. de C.V.
Pearson Education Malaysia Pte. Ltd.

10 9 8 7 6 5 4 3 2 1
ISBN: 0-13-117392-8

TABLE OF CONTENTS

PREFACE

Why This Booklet Was Developed

Like teaching itself, integrating technology into educational practice is challenging work, full of exciting opportunities and complex problems. *Educational Technology in Action* brings these challenges to life by providing a series of hypothetical technology integration exercises based on actual situations and events.

These real-world problems give educators opportunities to reflect on and apply concepts they have read about in *Integrating Educational Technology into Teaching* (Roblyer, 2003). Participating in this simulated problem-solving helps prepare readers for the real world of technology in schools.

Contents of the Booklet

This booklet features the Technology Integration Planning (TIP) Model introduced in Chapter 2 of *Integrating Educational Technology into Teaching*. Based on a systematic instructional design process, the TIP Model addresses problems and planning needs unique to using technology resources in teaching and learning. This information is presented in three parts, and two features are included to help readers understand and apply it:

- **Part I** – Chapter 1 gives an overview of the purpose of the TIP Model and each of its five phases. Chapters 2-6 focus on each phase in turn, along with exercises to provide insight into and practice on the underlying concepts.
- **Part II** – Chapters 7-10 introduce and provide practice in technology integration strategies for each of several technologies: instructional software, software tools, multimedia/hypermedia, and Internet/distance learning materials.
- **Part III** – Chapters 11-16 describe and provide exercises on technology integration strategies for six content areas: language arts/foreign languages, mathematics/science, social studies, art/music, physical education/health, and special education.
- **End-of-Part Review Exercises** – These are in the booklet at the end of each part and duplicated online at: **http://www.prenhall.com/roblyer**. Students will click on the *Educational Technology in Action* module and use the links in it to answer the questions.
- **Tutorials CD** – Instructional exercises in the booklet often refer to students creating or using Microsoft *Word* and Microsoft *Excel* documents, web pages, and *PowerPoint* presentations. The CD included with this booklet has sample step-by-step tutorials that give readers hands-on practice in using *Word, Excel, Netscape Composer,* and *PowerPoint* to design products for four of the curriculum lessons described in the exercises. (**NOTE:** The *Adobe Acrobat Reader*® required to view the tutorials is on the CD.)

Chapter Organization

Each chapter has the following components:

- **Introduction** – This section gives an overview of the chapter and a summary of the information required to solve the problems in the chapter.
- **Scenarios to Read and Analyze** – Each chapter has two scenarios in which decisions were made about technology-based policies, resources, applications, and planning steps. Each is followed by questions that ask readers to reflect on the decisions and analyze their impact.
- **Problems to Analyze and Solve** – Each chapter has five problems that ask readers to apply what they know about technology integration by imagining they are educators who must make decisions about technology integration. In each case, they tell what they think is appropriate to do.

NOTE: Readers may notice that most scenarios and problem exercises focus on middle and high school levels. Although the question of whether or not to emphasize technology uses at lower levels remains controversial, this booklet reflects the position that a greater number of demonstrably effective uses of technology are at middle and high school levels.

Correlation with Educational Technology Standards

The scenarios in Chapters 2-16 are designed to address ISTE's National Educational Technology Standards for Teachers (NETS-T). A listing of the NETS-T and the correlation chart are on the inside covers of this booklet.

Other Instructor Resources Available with This Booklet

Educational Technology in Action is one of a set of ancillary resources that expand on topics introduced in *Integrating Educational Technology into Teaching* (Roblyer, 2003). Its problem-based format can support introductory instructional technology courses, methods and issues courses, administrative methods courses, and workshops on technology integration. Readers may also find it helpful to use some or all of the following support materials packaged with the *Integrating Educational Technology into Teaching* textbook:

The Companion Website (CW) at http://www.prenhall.com/roblyer – A set of materials that includes a Syllabus Manager™ for the instructor, and, to support each chapter: a self-test of multiple-choice items, *PowerPoint* slides that outline chapter topics, a message board area and chat room on which students may post comments and exchange ideas with others in response to *Questions for Thought and Discussion* (Activity 3 at end of each textbook chapter), and a place to add to students' electronic portfolios.

Integrating Technology Across the Curriculum CD-ROM (ISBN: 0-13-042319-X) – A searchable database with over 550 technology integration ideas, stored by grade level, technology used, content area, and topic. Each entry is labeled according to ISTE National Educational Technology Standards (NETS) for Students it addresses. Each chapter has a suggested exercise with the CD.

 Starting Out on the Internet: A Learning Journey for Teachers (ISBN: 0-13-110970-7) – Reviews basic Internet concepts for teachers and has interactive activities students do on the CW.

 The Computerized Test Bank (CTB) – A variety of test-item formats (multiple choice, true-false, short answer, essay) for each chapter.

Educational Technology in Action: Problem-based Exercises for Technology Integration – This booklet includes:

- **Scenarios to Guide Whole-class Discussion** – Focus on issues and steps specific to a phase of technology integration or integration strategies for a type of technology resource or a content area. Everyone reads the scenario and the instructor uses the questions that follow it to initiate and structure class discussion.

- **Problems for Small-Group Work** – Can be used to check individual knowledge, but are most useful when assigned to small groups of students to discuss and analyze. The questions after each problem help focus the discussion on important concepts.

- **Tutorial CD** – Students get individual hands-on practice in creating the products discussed in some of the exercises.

How to Use This Booklet With Other Instructor Resources

For instructors teaching with the *Integrating Educational Technology into Education* (*IETT*) textbook, the following sequence is recommended to make use of these resources:

Step 1: Students read the chapter and take CW Self-Test

The CW self-test is a great way for students to review information in each chapter to make sure they have read and remembered important concepts.

Step 2: Introduce the chapter topics with CW *PowerPoint* Slides

The instructor can use the slides on the CW to introduce the topics in class or ask the students to review them before class. This sets the stage for the hands-on work in the class.

Step 3: Use *Educational Technology in Action* in combination with *IETT*'s end-of-chapter individual and collaborative activities for in-class and homework learning activities

To guide meaningful learning, instructors can use this booklet in conjunction with the Collaborative Activities in *IETT*'s end-of-chapter exercises. Instructors can do some of the exercises in class and assign additional ones for homework. Use these two resources in the following way:

- Use exercises in Part I of this booklet *in place of* the Collaborative Activities for *IETT*'s Chapter 2 (page 48).

- Use exercises in Part II of this booklet *to supplement* Collaborative Activities in *IETT*'s Chapters 4-9. Instructors may choose some or all of the exercises.

- Have each student choose *one* of *IETT*'s Chapters 10-15 for further study. They do the chapter exercises in this booklet associated with the *IETT* chapter they choose.

- Have students do the products in the Tutorials CD as individual homework exercises to give them hands-on practice in creating technology products.

Step 4: Students do CD-ROM and CW Exercises outside class

For after-class homework, the book includes end-of-chapter exercises students do with the *Integrating Technology Across the Curriculum* CD, and Questions for Thought and Discussion they do on the CW Message Board.

Step 5: Assign CTB and Portfolio activities as final assessments

Two kinds of activities can be useful for final course assessments: the Computerized Test Bank (CTB) and the Portfolio activities. Instructors may choose to have students do these at the end of Parts (e.g., once a month or so), or at the end of each chapter, if time allows.

Acknowledgments

As American entrepreneur Henry Kaiser said, "Problems are only opportunities in work clothes." Preparing this booklet of problems about technology integration presented two kinds of opportunities. As a professional in the field of educational technology, I was challenged to scrutinize even more carefully the issues and decisions each teacher must confront when considering when and how to use technology in a classroom. For those who use this booklet as part of their teacher preparation program, it offers compelling and convincing insights made possible by reading the stories of others – always a powerful way to learn.

Yet let us not downplay the "work clothes" aspect of these opportunities. Writing this "little booklet" was like creating a small, populated world, complete with descriptions of personalities and their environments. Suffice it to say, it took longer than six days. In its pages, teachers will recognize even more clearly the work involved in using technologies. Learning new ways of enhancing one's teaching is one thing; finding time to do it is quite another! Yet these all are opportunities that cannot be ignored. Choosing to respond to them is a *sine qua non* of excellence.

For giving me the opportunity to write this book, I am again indebted to my friend, mentor, and editor, Debbie Stollenwerk, and to other Merrill professionals who made it take shape and become a useful instructional product: JoEllen Gohr, Kim Lundy, Mary Morrill, and Dan Parker.

As always, I am grateful for the continuing support of my family, Bill and Paige Wiencke, and of friends such as Sherry Alter and Paul Belt, Marilyn and Herb Comet, Pat Gagné, Barbara Hansen, Megan Hurley, FJ and Maxine King, Sharon and Jon Marshall, Sharon Milner, Mary Ann Myers, Gwen McAlpine and Paul Zimmer, and Myrtle Parks. I welcome the opportunity to thank them once again for the continuing gifts of their love and friendship.

M. D. Roblyer

Part I:
Introducing the Technology Integration Planning (TIP) Model

Chapter 1
Overview of the TIP Model

Background on the TIP Model

The Technology Integration Planning (TIP) Model introduced in the textbook *Integrating Educational Technology into Teaching* (Roblyer, 2003) gives teachers a systematic way to address challenges involved in integrating technology into teaching. In each of the model's five phases, teachers perform a set of planning and implementation steps that help assure their technology use will be efficient and successful in meeting needs they identify. This section gives an overview of the five phases, describes the focus of each phase, and lists and explains issues teachers address at each stage.

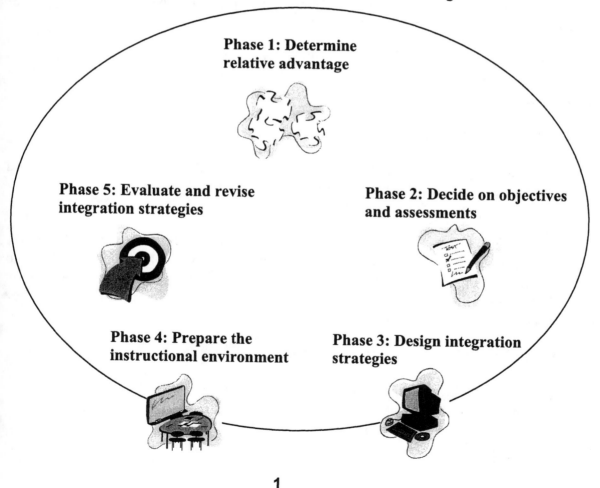

Phase 1: Determine relative advantage

Phase 5: Evaluate and revise integration strategies

Phase 2: Decide on objectives and assessments

Phase 4: Prepare the instructional environment

Phase 3: Design integration strategies

 **Phase 1: Determine relative advantage**

Focus: *Why should I use a technology-based method?* Teachers look at their current teaching problems and identify technology-based methods that may offer good solutions.

In his best-selling book on how and why innovations get adopted, Everett Rogers (*Diffusion of Innovation*, 1995) says that people resist changing how they do things, even if new ways are better. However, people are more likely to change if they see clearly the benefits of a new method over an old one. He calls this seeing a "relative advantage." The following make it easier to see relative advantage:

1. **Compatibility** – Methods consistent with their cultural values and beliefs and others adopted in the past. For example, teachers see using technology as compatible with their views of what it means to be a good teacher.

2. **Complexity** – Easy enough for them to learn and to carry out on a frequent basis. Teachers who use technology-based methods feel that they are both feasible to learn and not too time-consuming to do routinely.

3. **Trialability** – Being able to try it out a little before making a final decision.

4. **Observability** – Seeing others they respect or emulate using the new method successfully. For many teachers, observability is a kind of trialability, since they "try out" the method vicariously through other teachers or trainers.

At this Phase, teachers review their curriculum and teaching methods and identify instructional problems for which technology might offer a good solution. Trialability and observability help them review a technology-based method and determine if it is compatible with their values and easy enough for them to learn and implement. Then they make a decision on its relative advantage for them.

Summary of Issues to address in Phase 1:

* Are there any topics or curriculum objectives I have difficulty teaching?
* Do any of these instructional problem areas have technology-based solutions?
* What is the relative advantage of the technology-based solutions?
* Is the relative advantage sufficient to justify the effort involved?

Phase 2: Decide on objectives and assessments

Focus: *How will I know students have learned?* Teachers decide skills they want students to learn from the lesson(s) and design ways to assess how well students have learned and how effectively the activity has been carried out.

To be sure a technology successfully addressed the problems they identified in Phase 1, teachers state expectations in the form of observable, measurable outcomes, then design materials to measure outcomes. For many skills, teachers use traditional assessments (e.g., multiple choice, short answer, true-false, matching, essay). For more complex skills such as web site production work or cooperative group work, teachers may either design or acquire the following kinds of materials:

- **Performance checklists** – Lists of tasks students have to accomplish for credit. Performance checklists list tasks and points awarded for accomplishing them. For example, students get a point for carrying out each step an experiment.
- **Criterion checklists** – Lists of criteria students must meet in their work and products. If students must not only do tasks but also must do them to a certain level of quality, the criteria are listed with the point spread possible. For example, students must locate 10 web sites that meet stated criteria for 1-3 points each.
- **Rubrics** – A set of descriptions of levels of performance (e.g., low, medium, high) on each of several aspects of the product or activity (e.g., content quality). Look at the following web site to see example rubrics and use a template to help design them: **http://rubistar.4teachers.org/index.shtml**

Sometimes, teachers gather data through observations to see if desired behaviors are increasing. If they want to see if students are enjoying the new methods or have better attitudes toward the subject, they also may have a non-instructional outcome such as "Higher motivation to do group production work" and state an objective to define it. They usually design self-report instruments to measure these outcomes.

Summary of Issues to address in Phase 2:

- What kinds of performances do I expect from students to show they learned?
- What is the best way for me to assess students' learning progress and products: e. g., written tests (multiple choice, true-false, matching, short answer, essays), performance or criterion checklists, rubrics?
- Do the desired instruments exist or do I have to develop them?
- What other methods could gauge success (e.g., observations, attitude instruments)?

Phase 3: Design integration strategies

Focus: *What teaching strategies and activities will work best?* Teachers decide on instructional strategies and how to carry them out.

When teachers create an instructional design for technology integration, they consider the characteristics of their topic and the needs of their students and decide on an instructional course of action that addresses both within the constraints of their classroom environment. This means making decisions about:

- **Instructional approaches** – Teachers may teach topics in a traditional, directed manner: present new concepts, have students practice, test student knowledge. Inquiry-based (constructivist) approaches, on the other hand, require students to discover at least some concepts that were once just told to them. Decisions about which instructional approaches to use drives all other ones on curriculum, grouping, and sequence.
- **Curriculum approaches** – Some content areas once taught as separate topics (single subject approach) are now taught in combination (interdisciplinary approach). Some teachers feel that this better reflects real life, where a problem may call for applying skills in several content areas.
- **Grouping** – In some situations, individual students must learn and demonstrate mastery of skills. In others, teachers have the option to place students in pairs or small groups.
- **Sequence** – As teachers design the sequence of steps in the integration activity, they consider ways to encourage equity of technology use, as well as to make sure students have prerequisite technology skills that allow them to learn effectively from the resources.

Summary of Issues to address in Phase 3:

- Should activities be directed, constructivist, or a combination of these?
- Will the instruction be single subject or interdisciplinary?
- Should activities be individual, paired, small group, large group, whole class?
- What strategies should I use to encourage females and minority students to be integrally involved with the technologies?
- What sequence of activities should I teach?
- Have I built in demonstrations of the skills students will need to use both equipment and the specific software?
- Have I allowed students enough time to get used to materials before beginning a graded activity?

Phase 4: Prepare the environment

Focus: *Are essential conditions in place to support teaching and learning?* Teachers organize the teaching environment so technology plans can be carried out effectively.

Since research on effective technology uses shows that teachers can integrate technology successfully *only* if they have adequate hardware, software, and technical support available to them, the International Association for Technology in Education (ISTE NETS for Students, 2000) lists a set of *essential conditions* that are necessary to unleash the potential power of technology tools and methods. The school and district must provide many of these essential conditions, but for each technology integration strategy, the teacher considers which conditions are in place and to what degree. This helps shape the kind of integration possible for the situation. For example, if 30 computers would be ideal, but only five are available, the teacher adapts the plan accordingly.

Summary of Issues to address in Phase 4:

- How many computers and copies of software will be needed to carry out the activities?
- How many computers and copies of software are available?
- Over what time period and for how long will technology resources be needed?
- Do I need to schedule time in a lab or media center?
- If demonstrations and learning stations are to be used, will projection devices or large-screen monitors be needed?
- What other equipment, software, media, and resources will be needed (e.g., printers, software)?
- Have I checked out the legality of the uses I want to make?
- Have I provided for students' privacy and safety?
- Have I made all necessary access provisions for students with physical disabilities?
- Have I become familiar with troubleshooting procedures specific to the piece of hardware or software package being used? (Equipment and software manuals often list such procedures.)
- Have I built in time to test run an equipment setup before students arrive?
- Have I built in time to back up important files? Have I trained students to back up theirs?
- Do I have the original program disks/discs handy to reinstall them if necessary?
- Do I have a backup plan if I cannot use the resources as I had planned?

Phase 5: Evaluate and revise

Focus: *What worked well? What could be improved?* Teachers review outcome data and information on technology-integrated methods and determine what should be changed to make them work better next time.

In addition to collecting formal data on instructional and other outcomes, teachers sometimes interview students and observers to ask what they think could be improved. Some teachers keep daily notes or logs on implementation problems and issues. As they review all the information, teachers can use the following *Technology Impact Checklist* (Roblyer, 2003) to help them reflect on whether the problems they identified in Phase 1 have, indeed, been addressed successfully:

How Do You Know When You've Integrated Technology Well?
-An outside observer sees the technology activity as a seamless part of the lesson.
-The reason for using the technology is obvious to you, the students, and others.
-The students are focusing on learning, not on the technology.
-You can describe how technology is helping a particular student.
-You would have difficulty accomplishing lesson objectives if the technology weren't there.
-You can explain easily and concisely what the technology is supposed to contribute.
-All students are participating with the technology and benefiting from it.

How Do You Know When You HAVEN'T Integrated Technology Well?
-You consistently see the technology as more trouble than it's worth.
-You have trouble justifying cost and preparation time in terms of benefits to your students.
-Students spend more time trying to make the technology work than on learning the topic.
-The problem you were trying to address is still there.

Summary of Issues to address in Phase 5:

- Have I identified an instructional problem to solve?
- Have I identified types of evidence that will indicate to me whether or not the new strategy is solving or might help solve the problem?
- Have I solicited feedback from students about how to improve activities?
- Have I used instruments to collect data on the impact of the activity?
- Have I reviewed results and determined if the strategy has solved the problem or could solve the problem with changes?
- Have I considered alternative ways to set up equipment so activities go more smoothly?
- What do I need to change to achieve better impact?

Chapter 2

Problem-based Exercises on Phase 1 of the TIP Model:
Determining the Relative Advantage

Introduction to Phase 1 Concepts

Every teacher has topics – and sometimes whole subject areas – that they find especially challenging to teach. Some concepts are so abstract or foreign to students that they struggle to understand them; some topics students find so boring, tedious, or irrelevant that they have trouble attending to them. Some learning requires time-consuming tasks that students resist doing. Good teachers spend much time trying to meet these challenges and make concepts more engaging or easier to grasp, or make tasks more efficient to accomplish.

Recognizing relative advantage. Technology-based strategies offer many unique benefits to teachers as they look for instructional solutions to these problems. However, time and effort to plan and carry out technology-based methods and sometimes involves additional expense. Teachers have to consider the benefits of using such a method compared to their current ones and decide if the benefits are worth the additional effort and cost.

As described in Chapter 1 of this booklet, Everett Rogers (*Diffusion of Innovations*, 1995) refers to this decision as seeing the "relative advantage" for using a new method *Integrating Educational Technology into Teaching* (2003) lists several kinds of learning problems and technology solutions with potential for high relative advantage to teachers (pp. 43-44). However, these lists are merely general guidelines. Being able to recognize specific instances of these problems in a classroom context and knowing how to match them with an appropriate technology solution takes both practice and an in-depth knowledge of the characteristics of each technology.

This booklet provides some of the practice you will need, but to make this practice most helpful, first read in *Integrating Educational Technology into Teaching* about the features and applications of each technology before doing the practice problems in chapters 7-10 of this booklet. Also, before doing practice problems in chapters 11-16, read about problems and technology solutions specific to each content area.

Phase 1 questions. The first phase in integrating technology requires answering two questions about technology's relative advantage in a given situation. These questions are listed on the next page with suggestions for answering them in actual classroom situations.

1. **What is the problem I am addressing?** To make sure a technology application is a good solution, begin with a clear statement of a teaching and learning problem. This is sometimes difficult to do. It is a natural human tendency to jump to a quick solution rather than recognize the real problem. Also, everyone may not see a problem the same way. Use the following guidelines to answer the question of "what is the problem?"

- **Do not focus on technologies** – Remember that knowing how to use a technology appropriately is part of a *solution*, and is not in itself a *problem* to solve. Therefore, avoid problem statements like "Students do not know how to use spreadsheets efficiently" or "Teachers are not having their students use the Internet." Not having the skills to use a technology (e.g., a spreadsheet or the Internet) is an instructional problem, but not the kind of teaching/learning problem to consider here. It is sometimes true that teachers are given a technology and told to implement it. In these situations, they must decide if there is a real teaching or learning problem the new resource can help meet. However, if teachers have a technology available and choose not to use it, it may mean they can see no relative advantage to using it; non-use of a technology is not in itself a problem to address with the TIP Model.

- **Look for evidence** – Look for observable indications there really is a problem. Examples of evidence are: students consistently achieve lower grades on a skill area, a formal or informal survey shows that teachers have trouble getting students to attend to learning tasks, or teachers observe that students are refusing to turn in required assignments in a certain area.

2. **Do technology-based methods offer a solution with sufficient relative advantage?** Analyze the benefits of the technology-based method in light of the effort and cost to implement it and make a final decision. Use the following guidelines to answer the question of "Is technology a good solution?"

- **Estimate the impact** – Consider the benefits others have gained from using a technology as a solution. Is it likely you will realize similar benefits?

- **Consider the required effort and expense** – How much time and work will it take to implement the technology solution? Is it likely to be worth it?

The problem-based exercises in this chapter give you hands-on practice in applying Phase 2 of the TIP Model concepts you read in Chapter 1. Through scenario-based problem situations, you see how teachers go about answering these key questions by using trialability and observability to determine the complexity, compatibility, and relative advantage of technology-based solutions.

Scenarios to Read and Analyze – Read each scenario and answer the questions after it using information you read in Chapter 1 about the TIP Model:

Scenario 1, Phase 1 – Mia and Lars, teachers from two different high schools, were discussing strategies for including multicultural activities in the social studies curriculum.

"I'm thinking of trying something new this year," said Mia. "Our principal gives us travel money to go to a conference or workshop each year, so this year I went to a workshop at the Highmarkes School District. They described an online project with partner schools in countries all over the world. One teacher told about her partners in Israel and Spain. She said students exchange information with designated partners and answer assigned questions to research each other's backgrounds and locales. Then they work in groups on travel brochures or booklets to e-mail each other. They even take digital photos of each other and scan pictures from school yearbooks. It sounded like a great way for my kids to learn about other cultures while they learn geography and civics."

"Wow," said Lars. "It's great your principal does that; our principal doesn't. But that project sounds like a lot of trouble. Would you have to do it all yourself?"

"Our library-media center has a technology resource guy that helps us when we run into technical problems," said Mia. "And, you know, most of us at my school have Internet connections in our classrooms now."

"We're still waiting for that in my school," said Lars. "My classes usually look in books for information on assigned countries and do a research paper or poster. However, they do bring in foods from their own cultures. Last year, we had a smorgasbord with five or six different authentic cuisines. What great egg rolls!"

Mia nodded, "Yes, I've done that, too, and they do seem to enjoy it. I don't think it makes much of an impression, though, as far as appreciating other cultures. I still hear a lot of racial epithets used in the halls, and jokes about students' color or race-specific characteristics – real and imagined."

Lars shook his head, "Well, I don't think there's much we can do about that."

"Maybe not," sighed Mia, "but it's sure harder to demean people from other cultures when you've really worked with them and gotten to know them. I thought I'd give this way a try. The teacher from Highmarkes said she'd help me get started. I thought I'd go over and visit her class to see how she organizes it."

"Well," said Lars. "I'd be interested to hear if you think it's worth the trouble."

S1.1   What relative advantages does Mia see for the technology-based approach – i.e., in what ways does she seem to think it might be better than her previous one?

S1.2   How did trialability and observability help Mia see the relative advantage?

S1.3   Why do you think Lars doesn't see the relative advantage?

S1.4   What do you think might help persuade Lars of the relative advantage?

Scenario 2, Phase 1 – Leroy was a veteran middle school science teacher in a large, suburban school district. Despite the many awards he had won for his teaching, he was becoming increasingly dissatisfied with the way students were learning science in his school. He felt that, despite his efforts to make his class hands-on and project-based, his students tended to see science as facts and procedures unrelated to real-life problems. Other teachers in the school taught science in an even more traditional way than he did, with limited group projects and hands-on experiments. He felt most students left middle school without learning the usefulness of scientific inquiry.

One day, he attended a science conference where he heard a university professor and a science teacher presenting software they had designed and used with middle school students. The software began with a video problem scenario presented as it if were a real live newscast. The video said that an alien spaceship was orbiting earth and broadcasting a plea for help. Aliens on board were from several planets in a galaxy whose sun had exploded. They escaped but now needed new habitats that would meet the needs of their various species. They asked earth for help in matching them with planets and moons each might find habitable. (*See end of chapter note.)

The conference presenters went on to tell about the rich, inquiry-based environment the software provided and the teacher support materials that came with it. There were built-in information banks about planets and their moons, probes they could design and "send out" to collect data, daily lesson plans, suggestions for grouping – even practice test items and rubrics for judging products. They said the software had drawn students into activities that helped them learn scientific inquiry approaches, rather than isolated facts and steps.

The whole idea of integrating this kind of activity into science instruction fired Leroy's imagination. He decided to have his students do this for his solar system unit instead of building models of planets. If it worked well, he would try getting other teachers to adopt it and would look for other project-based software simulations they could use. When he got back to town, he invited Arvella, district science coordinator, to his school to see the demo he had gotten at the conference.

"Whew! This looks complicated, Leroy!" said Arvella. Are you sure the kids can do this? Don't you think it might frustrate them – all these probes and stuff?"

"I don't think so," said Leroy. "I'll bet they get it faster than the teachers do."

"Hmm," said Arvella, "if it works, we could build it into district curriculum."

S2.1   What kind of relative advantage does Leroy see for this software – i.e., how will it address the problems he has identified?

S2.2   Why does Leroy feel it would meet his needs better than model building?

S2.3   Why did Arvella view the activity differently than Leroy?

S2.4   Assuming it works well, would requiring it in the curriculum be a good way of showing other teachers the relative advantage of using this software?

Phase 1 Problems to Analyze and Solve

P.1. You are a high school mathematics teacher. At a faculty meeting, your principal announced that the district had purchased a site license for an SAT preparation program. He said that any teacher could obtain a copy of the software for use in the classroom by attending a Saturday training program that the district will hold.

P1.1 What kinds of benefits to your students and to you would motivate you to consider using the software, and how could you find out about them?

P.1.2 What experiences could provide the trialability and observability to help you decide if using this software had relative advantage for you, and how would you go about obtaining these experiences?

P.1.3 What could the district and/or principal do to help you decide?

P.2. You are a third grade teacher and are talking with another third grade teacher in her classroom. She shows you how she uses spreadsheets to demonstrate math concepts such as graphing data from a table of numbers. She says has been using spreadsheet software to keep her home budgets and she realized how visual it made math concepts, so she started using it with some of her math lessons. You have never used spreadsheets, but you are interested in the approach she is using.

P2.1 What problem does the spreadsheet activity seem to be addressing?

P2.2 What kinds of questions would you ask her to help you decide if this activity would have relative advantage for you and your students?

P2.3 Why might this activity have more immediate relative advantage for her than for you?

P.3. Scores on the state's test of writing skills are unusually low for your district's eighth graders, and a university English education professor has been hired as a consultant to help improve them. At a one-day staff development workshop, the professor describes how having students write e-mails to students at other sites can motivate them to write more and want to improve their writing style and mechanics. After the workshops, several teachers complain among themselves that the method is worthless and that the day had been a waste of their time.

P3.1 What did the professor assume about the causes of students' writing problems?

P3.2 What are some reasons this may not have been the best way to demonstrate the relative advantage of this approach?

P3.3 What might be a better way to explore whether or not this method had relative advantage over the way teachers currently teach writing?

P.4. The superintendent of the Wellmade School District felt that every student should be "connected to the Information Superhighway," so he decided to install Internet connections in every school classroom in the district. The hardware and installations were funded through a federal grant and local business sponsors. Two years later, it became apparent that only about 25% of the teachers were using the Internet with students, and most uses were "casual surfing."

P4.1 Why do you think the teachers did not see the relative advantage of this technology?

P4.2 If you were made responsible for integrating this technology into instructional activities, how would you translate the superintendent's rationale into problems and solutions the teachers could understand?

P4.3 How would you use trialability and observability to help teachers see the relative advantage of this innovation?

P.5. The principal of a high school visited a school district where all teachers used handheld computers to assess students as they worked on small group projects. Teachers were able to take notes as they walked around the classroom; then they downloaded the notes to their own classroom computer workstations, where it could be graded and printed out. The teachers seemed to feel this resource was a time-saver and helped them do instructional activities they couldn't do before. Your principal comes to you, the lead science teacher in the school, and asks you if you think you and other teachers would like to have handheld computers.

P5.1 What information would you need to make a decision about the relative advantage of this resource?

P5.2 How could the principal help you obtain the information you need?

P5.3 What would you need to know about the complexity and compatibility of this technology before you could answer the principal's question?

---

* **NOTE:** Scenario 2 is based upon an actual award-winning software package called *Alien Rescue*, designed as a collaborative project of the University of Texas at Austin, the University of Louisiana at Lafayette, and Texas A&M University. Anyone interested in learning more about this software may contact Dr. Susan Pedersen at: spedersen@coe.tamu.edu.

Chapter 3

Problem-based Exercises on Phase 2 of the TIP Model: *Deciding on Objectives and Assessments*

Introduction to Phase 2 Concepts

Writing objectives is a good way of setting clear expectations for what technology-based methods will accomplish. Usually, teachers expect a new method will improve *student behaviors*, e.g., better achievement, more on-task behaviors, improved attitudes. Sometimes, however, changes in *teacher behaviors* are important, e.g., saving time on a task. In either case, objectives should focus on *outcomes* that are observable (e.g., demonstrating, writing, completing), rather than internal ones that cannot be seen or measured (e.g., being aware, knowing, understanding, or appreciating).

After stating objectives, teachers create ways to assess how well outcomes have been accomplished. Sometimes, they can use existing tests and rubrics. For others, they have to create instruments or methods to measure the behaviors.

Example outcomes, objectives, and assessments. Here are a few examples of outcomes, objectives to state them in a measurable form, and assessment methods matched to them:

- **Higher achievement outcome:** Overall average performance on an end-of-chapter test will improve by 20%. (Assess achievement with a test.)

- **Cooperative work outcome:** All students will score at least 15 out of 20 on the cooperative group skill rubric. (Use an existing rubric to grade skills.)

- **Attitude outcome:** Students will indicate satisfaction with the simulation lesson by an overall average score of 20 of 25 points. (Create an attitude survey to assess satisfaction.)

- **Improved motivation:** Teachers will observe better on-task behavior in at least 75% of the students. (Create and use an observation sheet.)

Phase 2 questions. This phase in integrating technology requires answering two questions about outcomes and assessment strategies. These questions are listed on the next page with suggestions for answering them in actual classroom situations:

1. **What outcomes do I expect from using the new methods?** Think about problems you are trying to solve and what would be acceptable indications that the technology solution has succeeded in resolving them. Use the following guidelines:

- **Focus on results, not processes** – Think about the *end results* you want to achieve, rather than the *processes* to help you get there. Avoid statements like "Students will learn cooperative group skills" which tells a process students use to achieve the outcome (improved cooperative group skills). Instead, state what you want students to be able to do as a result of the multimedia project, for example "90% of students will score 4 out of 5 on a cooperative groups skills rubric."
- **Make statements observable and measurable** – Avoid vague statements that cannot be measured like "Students will understand how to work cooperatively."

2. **What are the best ways of assessing these outcomes?** The choice of assessment depends on the nature of the outcome. See the following guidelines:

- **Use written tests to assess skill achievement outcomes** – Written cognitive tests (e.g., short answer, multiple choice, true-false, matching) and essay exams remain the most common classroom assessment strategy for many formal knowledge skills.
- **Use evaluation criteria checklists to assess complex tasks or products** – When students must create complex products such as multimedia presentations, reports, or web pages, teachers may give students a set of criteria that specify requirements each product must meet. Points are awarded for meeting each criterion.
- **Use rubrics to assess complex tasks or products** – Rubrics fulfill the same role as evaluation criteria checklists and are sometimes used in addition to them. Their added value is giving students descriptions of various levels of quality. Teachers usually associate a letter grade with each level of quality (Level 5 = A, Level 4 = B, etc.).
- **Use surveys or semantic differentials to assess attitude outcomes** – When the outcome is improved attitudes, teachers either design a list of survey questions for students to answer or have students react to a question (e.g., "How do you feel about math?") by checking a line between each of several sets of bipolar adjectives to indicate their level of feeling (e.g., "Warm _ _ _ _ _ Cold? Happy _ _ _ _ _ Sad?")
- **Use observation instruments to measure frequency of behaviors** – For example, if teachers wanted to see an increase in students' use of scientific language, they could create a chart to keep track of this use on a daily basis.

Problem-based exercises in this chapter give you hands-on practice in applying Phase 2 of the TIP Model concepts. Through scenario-based problem situations, you see how teachers go about deciding on appropriate outcomes, stating objectives, and matching good assessment strategies to them.

Scenarios to Read and Analyze – The following scenarios are continuations of the ones begun in Chapter 2. Answer the questions using information you have read about Phase 2 of the TIP Model in the Introduction to this chapter and in Chapter 1:

Scenario 1, Phase 2 – Mia was so impressed with the online project at Highmarkes School District, she decided to try it out in her own classroom. She reflected on the problems she saw with her current methods of addressing multicultural awareness and what she wanted her students to learn about other cultures that they didn't seem to be learning now. She decided on the following outcomes: better attitudes toward people of other cultures, increased learning about similarities and differences among cultures, skills in using the Internet and e-mail for communication, and positive attitudes toward instruction. She created these objectives to measure the outcomes:

- **Attitudes toward cultures:** At least 75% of students will demonstrate an improved attitude toward the culture being studied by achieving a higher score on an attitude measure after the Internet activity than before.
- **Knowledge of cultures:** Each student group will score at least 90% on a rubric on a brochure or booklet that reflects knowledge of the characteristics (both unique and common to our own) of the language, geography, people, governments and other information about the culture being studied.
- **Internet skills:** At least 90% of students will demonstrate they can independently do 95% of listed skills on e-mail, browsers, and search engine use.

For the last outcome, she wasn't sure what to require and decided to ask her colleague Lars if he knew of any good measures. For other outcomes, she designed:

- **Semantic differential:** She knew a good way to measure attitudes was with set of adjectives with lines between them: EX: cruel _ _ _ _ _ kind). Before and after the project, students answer a question like "How do you feel about people from ____?" by marking a line between the adjectives to indicate how they feel.
- **Knowledge of cultures:** After listing all the characteristics she wanted to see reflected in their products, she created a rubric to assess them.
- **Internet skills:** She listed the skills and created a checklist handout of them.

S1.1 Add bipolar adjectives and create a sheet for a semantic differential instrument that Mia might use to assess attitudes toward other cultures.

S1.2 What are some features you think should be assessed in the product rubric?

S1.3 If you were Lars, how would you advise Mia to state the fourth outcome?

S1.4 What instrument or method would you advise her to select or create to assess how well the fourth outcome had been accomplished?

Scenario 2, Phase 2 – Leroy decided to use in his science classroom the inquiry-based software he had learned about at the conference. As he thought about what he wanted to achieve with this new method, he made mental comparisons of how students currently viewed learning science and how he wanted them to look at it. He decided that, in addition to passing his usual test on solar system information, he wanted students to achieve the following outcomes: demonstration of problem solving approach to assigned problems, ability to create new problems to solve and design methods to solve them, increased transfer of the language of scientific inquiry to tasks outside the aliens unit, and increased enjoyment of using scientific inquiry methods. He developed the following objectives to measure the outcomes:

- **Problem solving approaches:** All students working in small groups will create well-designed problem statements, solutions steps, and workable solutions for at least 1 of 3 problems assigned.
- **New problem creation:** At least 75% of groups will be able to generate at least one new problem to explore related to the alien simulation software.
- **Scientific inquiry language use transfer:** At least 80% of students will be heard using the language of scientific inquiry outside the unit.

He wasn't sure how to deal with the "science enjoyment" outcome and decided to ask district science coordinator Arvella how she would state and assess this outcome. For the other assessments, he decided on the following:

- **Problem solving criterion checklist:** He decided to use the software Teacher Manual's checklist of steps students should complete and criteria they should meet for each step.
- **Problem creation rubric:** He designed a rubric based on a list of features that well-designed problems should reflect.
- **Scientific language observation instrument:** He designed an observation instrument with students' names and a daily checklist. Each day he would check off names of students he or others had observed using the terms or phrases that indicated use of inquiry approaches.

S2.1 Leroy wonders if he has set the criteria for success too low in the first outcome objective. What features of the situation might help him decide on good criteria?

S2.2 What features might you include in a rubric to assess well-designed problems?

S2.3 If you were Arvella, how would you tell Leroy to state an "enjoyment" outcome?

S2.4 What kind of instrument or method would you advise Leroy to select or create to assess the "science enjoyment" outcome?

Phase 2 Problems to Analyze and Solve

P1. You are a middle school language arts teacher. You would like to have your students begin word-processing their written stories and compositions instead of writing them by hand or typing them. Right now, they write as little as possible, and getting them to make corrections is always like pulling teeth. You hope word processing will increase the amount they write and make them more likely to revise their work based on your feedback at least once for each written product.

P1.1 How would you state an outcome objective about increasing the amount students write?

P1.2 How would you state an outcome objective about getting students to make corrections?

P1.3 What would be a good way to assess these two outcomes?

P2. You are a guidance counselor who would like junior level students to use new software the state has provided to help them prepare for the state graduation test. You feel that using this software even an hour a week will raise students' scores as much as 20% across the junior class.

P2.1 How would you state the objective for this performance outcome?

P2.2 Would you consider any increase less than 20% as an adequate indication of the software's usefulness for juniors? How could you reflect this in the objective statement?

P2.3 What would you use to assess how well this objective was accomplished?

P.3 You are a high school French teacher who wants students to have a "language immersion" learning experience, yet you and your students cannot afford to travel to a French-speaking locale. You decide to try a "virtual immersion experience" by having your students visit French language web sites and locate information to prepare a product in French (e.g., a brochure about a vacation spot in a French-speaking location, a restaurant menu with French descriptions and prices). You feel this activity will improve translation test scores and encourage students to use the French language in classroom conversation.

P3.1 How would you state an objective for an "improved translation test scores" outcome?

P3.2 How would you state an objective for the "increased French conversation" outcome?

P3.3 What would be a way to measure accomplishment of the second objective?

P4.   As a school district science coordinator, you would like the high school biology teachers to begin using a dissection simulation program in lieu of actual dissections of pigs, which has always been done in the past. You feel this will save both time and money for materials. Some biology teachers are reluctant to make this change; they say that students cannot learn as much about anatomy and dissection techniques from a simulation as they can from the "real thing." However, they agree to a test of the software in a couple classes.

P4.1   What would be the expectations of the simulation method in terms of general outcomes?

P4.2   If you were one of the biology teachers, how would you state objectives matched to these outcomes?

P4.3   What instruments or information would you use to assess the "saving time and money" objective?

P5.   You are a special education resource teacher for a school district. You attended a workshop about having students use presentation software (e.g., *PowerPoint*) for "book reports" and other summaries of works they have read. The workshop presenters say that students at all ability levels can use the software and find it more motivating to do such reports than regular written ones. Since you have heard complaints from teachers of gifted students and students with learning disabilities about how difficult it is to motivate students to do these reports, you would like to try this technique with both student groups. However, you are concerned that the students with disabilities might find the software frustrating.

P5.1   How would you state an outcome objective related to student motivation toward doing book reports?

P5.2   How would you state a different outcome objective related to use of the software by students with learning disabilities?

P5.3   What methods and materials would you use to assess these objectives?

Chapter 4

Problem-based Exercises on Phase 3 of the TIP Model: *Designing Integration Strategies*

Introduction to Phase 3 Concepts

Teachers make many design decisions as they integrate technologies into teaching, but the most important decision is whether the methods students will use to learn should be primarily directed (a teacher or expert source presents information for students to absorb) or primarily inquiry-based or constructivist (students do hands-on activities to generate their own learning). This decision usually drives all others about grouping, lesson sequence, and types of learning activities.

Deciding on teaching/learning methods. Use the following guidelines to help determine whether methods should be directed, inquiry-based, or a combination of both:

Choose directed methods when:	Choose inquiry-based methods when:
• It will be clear to students how they apply skills to real-world situations. • Students are highly motivated to learn the content. • Students are inexperienced in the topic and are not likely to have any knowledge base or prerequisite skills. • Students need to learn skills as quickly and efficiently as possible. • Content is concrete and unambiguous and lends itself to direct teaching.	• Students usually have problems seeing applications to real-world problems. • Students usually are unmotivated to learn content in traditional ways. • Students have had previous experience with the topic and already have acquired some skills in the content. • There is adequate time for hands-on learning and assessment. • Content is abstract and difficult for learners to grasp without hands-on work.

Phase 3 questions. This phase in integrating technology requires answering three questions about instructional strategies, technology materials, and implementation strategies. These questions are listed on the next page with suggestions for answering them in actual classroom situations:

1. **What kinds of instructional methods are needed in light of content objectives and student characteristics?** After using the guidelines listed on the previous page to decide whether the methods should be primarily directed or constructivist, also consider the following:

   - **Content approach** – Should the approach be single-subject or interdisciplinary? Sometimes school or district requirements dictate this decision, and sometimes teachers combine subjects into a single unit of instruction as a way to cover concepts and topics that they may not otherwise have time to teach. Most often, however, interdisciplinary approaches are used to model how real-life activities require using a combination of skills from several content areas.
   - **Grouping approach** – Should the students work as individuals, pairs, in small groups, or as a whole class? These decisions are made in light of how many computers or software copies are available, as well as the following guidelines:

     - **Whole class:** For demonstrations or to guide whole-class discussion prior to student work
     - **Individual:** When students have to demonstrate individual mastery of skills at the end of the lesson or project
     - **Pairs:** For peer tutoring; higher ability students work with those of lesser ability
     - **Small group:** To model real-world work skills by giving students experience in cooperative group work

2. **How can technology best support these methods?** Think about how you will carry out the technology-based solution you identified in Phase 2.

3. **How can I prepare students adequately to use technologies?** When designing a sequence of activities that incorporates technology tools, be sure to leave enough time for demonstrating tools to students and allowing them to become comfortable using them before they do a graded product.

After you have considered all these aspects, create a sequence of steps and a timeline for carrying out the lesson or project.

Problem-based exercises in this chapter give you hands-on practice in applying Phase 3 of the TIP Model concepts you read about in Chapter 1. Actual classroom application requires in-depth knowledge about capabilities of technology resources and their uses in content areas. However, exercises in this chapter focus on fundamental instructional decisions that are common to all content areas and that are required for effective integration of any technologies.

Scenarios to Read and Analyze – The following scenarios are continuations of the ones begun in Chapter 2. Answer the questions using information you have read about Phase 3 of the TIP Model in the Introduction to this chapter and in Chapter 1:

Scenario 1, Phase 3 – Mia knew that the changes she wanted to bring about in students' attitudes toward other cultures could not be done by telling them information and testing them on it. They would need to draw their own conclusions by working and communicating with people from other cultures. However, she felt many of the technical skills for Internet and e-mail use could be taught in a fairly directed way, since students would be motivated to use the most efficient methods to communicate with others and to obtain information for their products. Practice with these skills throughout the project would give them the level of mastery they needed.

She decided that students should work in groups of four with designated tasks for each person in the group. The project web site had some good suggestions on how to assign tasks and organize group work. It also had the following suggested sequence of activities for introducing and carrying out the project.

- **Step 1:** Sign up on project web site; obtain partner school assignments.
- **Step 2:** Teachers in partner schools contact each other and exchange notes on organizing instruction.
- **Step 3:** Teachers organize classroom resources for work on project.
- **Step 4:** Introduce project to students: display project information from project web site and discuss previous products done by other sites.
- **Step 5:** Assign students to groups; discuss task assignments with all members.
- **Step 6:** Teach beginning e-mail and Internet skills, if necessary.
- **Step 7:** Students do initial e-mail contacts/chats and introduce each other.
- **Step 8:** Teacher works with groups to identify information for final product.
- **Step 9:** Students do Internet searches to locate required information; take digital photos and scan required images; exchange information with partner sites.
- **Step 10:** Students do production work; exchange final products with partners.
- **Step 11:** Do debriefing and assessments of student work.

1.1 Are Mia's activities inquiry-based (constructivist), directed, or a combination of both? Explain.

1.2 What items would you need to cover with your "partner teacher" to coordinate instructional activities for the project?

1.3 What teacher-directed methods could you use to introduce e-mail/browser/search engine skills efficiently?

1.4 What could you include on the list of "required information for final product" to assure students learned geography, history, and biology/botany about the area?

Scenario 2, Phase 3 – Leroy realized that his students would learn inquiry-based methods only by seeing them in action and practicing them over time. His methods would have to be designed to facilitate, rather than direct, student learning and to encourage them to think on their own. He felt this project would be a good way for students to begin learning these complex skills, but he also knew the unit would take them more time than usual as they became used to new ways of thinking about science and about learning itself.

He also realized that students had to be prepared to answer conceptual and factual questions about the solar system on the state's required exams, so he would have to provide some diagnostic testing over these concepts and facts and, if necessary, some remedial practice. Luckily, the software Teacher Manual (TM) provided test items like this to cover background information, and he could supplement them with some of his own.

With these things in mind, he reviewed the software's Teacher Manual for how to keep the activity on track and created the following sequence of project activities:

- **Day 1:** Assign students to groups and assign one student from each group to log on computers with other members watching. Show them how to run the opening video. Allow them to explore the software environment on their own.
- **Day 2:** Have class review the problem by asking the probing questions listed in the TM. Allow groups to explore software further to answer any questions they don't remember answers to from first day.
- **Days 3-5:** Hold discussions about how they will collaborate and use inquiry approach to solve the problems. They develop their own inquiry problem statements. Demonstrate software features they will need. Students practice using them and define lists of alien needs.
- **Days 6-10:** Students use software features to explore planets and moons and develop hypotheses about best matches for each alien species.
- **Days 11-13:** Groups present their findings on best places for each species. Groups write up final selections in required format.
- **Days 14-16:** Final reflections, assessments, remedial practice, where necessary.

S2.1 Where might Leroy incorporate writing assignments to make this project more interdisciplinary?

S2.2 What strategies would you suggest Leroy build in to make sure girls are as involved as boys in the project?

S2.3 If some students demonstrated that they needed review of solar systems concepts, can you think of a fun, creative way they could do this on Days 15-16?

S2.4 At what point would you suggest Leroy introduce the idea of generating new problems to explore using the software resources?

Phase 3 Problems to Analyze and Solve

P1. Harriet is a high school AP composition teacher. She wants her students to do more spelling and grammar proofreading of their own written work and make required revisions on these items before turning papers in to her for grading. She feels word processing features will help them learn this habit, so she introduces the software to them in class. They have never used word processing before, but she feels AP students can learn word processing on their own. After a demonstration of word processing features on Monday, she tells them to go to the computer lab the next two class periods, do a word-processed paper, and turn it in to her at the end of the class period Wednesday. When she grades the papers, she realizes they are far worse than usual. Not only are ideas not as well-developed, spelling and grammar are worse. She decides the whole idea was a failure.

P1.1   What reasons related to Harriet's teaching sequence might explain this failure?
P1.2   Why do you think ideas in student papers were not as well-developed as usual?
P1.3   What are two things you suggest she do differently if she tries this again?

P2. You are a geometry teacher for gifted ninth grade students. They do well on end-of-chapter tests, but you want them to develop more insight on the practical applications of geometry in daily life. The book you are using has Internet enrichment activities that call for students to work together in small groups to identify such applications. You decide to do these enrichment activities in one class period at the end of the unit to try it out.

P2.1   Do your methods for integrating the enrichment activities need to be primarily directed or inquiry-based?
P2.2   What would you have to do when you introduce these Internet-based enrichment activities to make sure they were successful?
P2.3   Do you think one class period for the activities will be okay? Why or why not?

P3. Juan is an elementary teacher who has his young students use a software package that encourages thinking about problem solving. It calls for them to build simulated products that match an example product on the screen. After having them work in small groups to build several products, he asks them to reflect on and explain their methods for solving the problems.

P3.1   Are Juan's methods directed, inquiry-based, or a combination? Explain.
P3.2   What could he do to make sure boys don't dominate the "building activities?"
P3.3   What must Juan do before students use the software for the first time?

P4.   Luella is a language arts teacher who uses a software package with vocabulary practice items to improve students' performance on a college entrance exam. Before she has them use the software, she describes test-taking tips and strategies and then shows them how to use the software. Since she feels students can help each other with difficult words, she has them work in groups of three to practice the software. They take turns practicing for about 15 minutes at the end of each class period for the last two weeks of the grading period.

P4.1   Are Luella's methods primarily directed or inquiry-based?

P4.2   Do you think this group-based strategy is a good one for the activity? Why or why not?

P4.3   Do you think 15 minutes of group practice at the end of each class period will be enough to increase students' performance? Why or why not?

P5.   You are a middle school science teacher who wants to get his students more used to solving problems that require collecting and analyzing data. You decide to have them use new Microcomputer-based Labs (MBL's) the school has bought. The MBL's are handheld computers with sensors connected to them to measure light, temperature, voltage, movement, and speed. You plan an experiment where they collect temperature of various items under inside and outside conditions. Then they download the data to a computer in the classroom and chart the data to detect trends. You have 32 students, but there are only 8 MBL's. You plan to have them work in groups and you assign various roles for each student in the group.

P5.1   Are the methods you will use directed, inquiry-based, or a combination? Explain.

P5.2   What could you do to make sure boys don't dominate the actual data collection use of the available MBL's?

P5.3   What will you have to do before students use the MBL's to collect data "in the field" for the first time?

Chapter 5

Problem-based Exercises on Phase 4 of the TIP Model:
Preparing the Instructional Environment

Introduction to Phase 4 Concepts

If teachers could obtain all the teaching resources they needed whenever they wanted them, they would make all Phase 4 planning decisions after they had decided on best instructional strategies in Phase 3. In practice, teachers make many Phase 3 and 4 decisions at the same time. Most teachers usually decide how they will teach something in light of what they have available to teach it.

Essential conditions for effective technology uses. In Phase 4, teachers make sure their instructional environment meets all of the following essential conditions required for successful technology integration:

- **Adequate hardware, software, and media** – Enough computers are available and there are sufficient legal copies of instructional resources.

- **Time to use resources** – Hardware and enough legal copies of software have been obtained or scheduled for the time needed.

- **Special needs of students** – Provisions have been made for access by students with disabilities and for all students' privacy and safety.

- **Planning for technology use** – Teachers are familiar enough with the hardware and software to use it efficiently and do necessary troubleshooting; they have allowed time for testing and backup of files; they have a backup plan in the event technology resources fail to work as planned.

Phase 4 questions. This phase in integrating technology requires answering three questions about preparing an instructional environment that will support technology integration. These questions are listed on the next page with suggestions for answering them in actual classroom situations:

1. **What equipment, software, media, and materials will I need to carry out the instructional strategies?** As you create ways to stretch scarce resources, be sure that your strategies are ethical and in keeping with the reasons you chose a technology-based solution in the first place. Some guidelines:

- **Computers:** If enough computers aren't available to support the individual format you wanted, consider organizing the integration plan around student pairs or small groups. Also consider having computer and non-computer learning stations that individuals or groups cycle through, completing various activities at each one. However, if students must master skills on an individual basis, consider scheduling time in a computer lab when all students in the class can use resources at once.
- **Copies of software and media:** Unless a software or media package specifically allows it, making copies of published software or media is illegal, even if copies are used on a temporary basis. Inquire about education-priced lab packs and site licenses.
- **Access to peripherals:** In addition to computers, remember to plan for adequate access to printers, printer paper, and any other needed peripherals (e.g., probes, handhelds).
- **Handouts and other materials:** Prepare and copy any necessary support materials. Unless learning to use the software without guidance is a goal of the project, consider creating summary sheets to remind students how to do basic operations.

2. **How should resources be arranged to support instruction and learning?**

- **Access by students with disabilities:** For students with visual or hearing deficits, consider software or adaptive devices created especially to address these disabilities.
- **Privacy and safety issues:** Students should never use the Internet without adult supervision and should never do unplanned chat sessions. If possible, firewall software should be used to prevent accidental access to inappropriate sites.

3. **What planning is required to make sure technology resources work well?**

- **Troubleshooting:** Computers, like all machines, will occasionally break down. Learn simple diagnostic procedures so you can correct some problems without assistance.
- **Test-runs and backup plans:** Leave sufficient time to learn and practice using resources before students use them, but also try out the resources again just before class begins. Have a backup plan in case something goes wrong at the last minute.

The problem-based exercises in this chapter give you hands-on practice in applying Phase 4 of the TIP Model concepts you read in Chapter 1. Through scenario-based problem situations, you see how teachers go about arranging classroom and other resources to support technology-based methods.

Scenarios to Read and Analyze – The following scenarios are continuations of the ones begun in Chapter 2. Answer the questions using information you have read about Phase 4 of the TIP Model in the Introduction to this chapter and in Chapter 1:

Scenario 1, Phase 4 – As soon as she realized her students would be able to participate in the Internet project, Mia began to get organized. First, she made a timeline of project activities, so she would know when her students needed to use computers. She made sure to build in enough time to demonstrate the project site and get students used to using the browser and search engine. Then she began the following planning and preparation activities:

- **Handouts for students** – To make sure groups knew the tasks each member should do, she created handouts of timelines and what should be accomplished at each stage of the project. She also made a checklist of information students were to collect and made copies so students could check off what they had done as they went. She got a list of technical skills and tips on using search engines and browser from the project web site. To keep track of who was using these skills adequately, she created a matrix checklist of the skills with all students' names on it. She wanted everyone to know how she would grade work, so she made copies of the assessment instruments (rubric and technical skills checklist) and gave them to the students.

- **Computer schedule** – She had a classroom workstation consisting of five networked computers, each with Internet connection, so she set up a schedule for small groups to use the computers. She knew that some students would need to scan pictures, download image files from the digital camera, and process them for sending to their partner schools, so she scheduled some additional time in the computer lab for this work. She thought that students could also do other work in the library/media center after school, if they needed still more time.

S1.1   Later, Mia remembered an additional planning step: how students would do production work on their products. What planning would she have to do to make this possible?

S1.2   If Mia wanted to do a demonstration and display of the project web site to the whole class at one time, what resource would she have to arrange for to do this?

S1.3   Mia was concerned that students didn't reveal too much personal information about themselves to their partner schools. What guidelines should she give them about information exchanges to protect their privacy and security?

S1.4   If the network or Internet access were interrupted for a day, what could Mia have them do to make good use of their time during this delay?

Scenario 2, Phase 4 – After reading the software Teacher Manual (TM) and reflecting on the presentation he had heard at the conference, Leroy decided to take the TM's advice and resist the tendency to over-direct students. He knew he had to keep to a timeline in order to complete the project on schedule, but he also realized that the software designers were warning that too much structure would work against the purpose and design of the software. Keeping this in mind, he began his planning:

- **Software skills** – The software was quite rich with features, tools, and resources, which Leroy found fascinating. However, he realized the software was so complex, he couldn't be expert on everything in it. In fact, he knew that some of his students would probably become more expert than he in a very short time! However, he wanted to become as familiar with it as possible so he could answer students' initial questions, so he went through it carefully and took notes.

- **Handouts** – The TM gave a chart to help students keep track of each species' needs. Leroy prepared a group task sheet and inserted this and other helpful notes.

- **Lesson planning** – Leroy was such a veteran in his content area, he usually didn't work from a lesson plan. However, this project was so new and different from his usual methods, he felt he needed to make daily notes. He left space for items he would add as his class progressed, so he would be even more prepared next time.

- **Software copies** – He knew the software was available to teachers only from the university who developed it. It was free, but he had to sign an agreement that only his class would be using it. He completed the paperwork and obtained the software. He made sure each copy worked on the equipment they had available.

- **Computer scheduling** – The trickiest part would be scheduling time on computers in the computer lab, since he had only one computer in his room. He arranged with the lab coordinator to have the lab on the days he needed it. He also spoke with the principal, who agreed to give him an extra computer for his room.

S2.1   One of the tasks students did to collect information was to design and send out space probes, which the TM said was a fairly complex activity. Why didn't Leroy create a directions sheet for them on how to do such a complex task?

S2.2   Why didn't Leroy feel he needed to know more than his students about all facets of the software?

S2.3   What should Leroy tell students who might want a copy of the software?

S2.4   Later, Leroy remembered he needed to do something to prepare for assessment at the end of the unit. Look back at Phase 3. What will he need to prepare?

Phase 4 Problems to Analyze and Solve

P.1.   Bill wants to use a commercial math software package to help his students practice solving real-life problems that require setting up algebra equations. He has a five-station license for the package. Students are at many levels with algebra skills; some are quite good at this kind of problem; others need a lot of time to figure out each one. He has 30 students in his class; however, he has only a three-computer workstation in his room.

P1.1   Another math teacher advises him to make enough copies for the computer lab and have his students use it there. Is this a good idea? Why or why not?

P1.2   Yet another math teacher advises him to have a three-team competition, where each team of 10 students does a "relay race" and tries to get the most problems correct in a class period. Is this a good idea? Why or why not?

P1.3   Can you think of any other creative approaches Bill might use to have all his students use the software there in his classroom, rather than the lab?

P.2.   Aubrey plans to use a science simulation software package to have his students gain experience with setting and testing complex hypotheses. He saw the software demonstrated at a workshop and ordered a copy. He plans to demonstrate it on his classroom computer and have the class work on the problems as a whole group. His class begins on September 10, and the software is due to arrive September 7.

P2.1   Do you see any problem with how Aubrey plans to use the software in his classroom?

P2.2   Can you think of another way to use it that might be more effective?

P2.3   What essential planning steps is Aubrey probably neglecting in this time frame?

P.3.   One of Leroy's (in Scenario 2) colleagues sees the science software and is very intrigued. He would like to use the software in his own classroom. He plans to use only one copy of the software on his classroom computer and says he will have students view the demo and solve the problems as a whole class.

P3.1   In light of what you read in Scenario 2, would it be okay for Leroy to give him one copy? Why or why not?

P3.2   If you were Leroy, what would be the best way you could help your colleague?

P3.3   In light of what you read about the software designer's intent, do you think his colleague has a good plan for using the software? Why or why not?

P.4.   Sally is a language arts teacher who wants her students to word-process the poems they are writing for her poetry unit. She has three computers in her classroom. However, the principal wants to control use of paper in the school, so Sally has no classroom printer. She plans to have her students do a written draft of the poems at home, then come in and enter them into the computers. Then Sally will transfer the poems to disk, take them to the computer lab and print them out, and bring the copies back for students to work on further.

P4.1   Is Sally's plan a feasible one? Why or why not?

P4.2   Can you think of another way to plan for printing when she has no printer in the room?

P4.3   Do you think it is a good idea to have students do written drafts first before they do them on word processing? Why or why not?

P.5.   Esmerelda is having her students do a social studies project where they do "virtual interviews" of experts on various periods in U.S. history. She schedules time in the computer lab and has them locate experts by searching Internet sites. She gives them an initial list of sites, but encourages them to branch out from there, looking for additional sites on their own. There is no lab manager and she has to go back to the classroom for periods of time as they work, but she knows they are competent Internet users and can be trusted not to leave the lab without permission. For their contacts with experts, she has them prepare a standard e-mail with the school name; their names, ages, addresses, and personal e-mail address, if they have one; and a description of what they would like to know.

P5.1   Assuming she is correct that students will not leave the lab with permission, is Esmeralda's plan for having students use the Internet a good one? Why or why not?

P5.2   Do you see any problems with the e-mail she is having them send?

P5.3   How would you change her plan to improve it?

Chapter 6

Problem-based Exercises on Phase 5 of the TIP Model: *Evaluating and Revising Integration Strategies*

Introduction to Phase 5 Concepts

As teachers complete a technology-based project with students, they begin reviewing evidence on how successful the strategies and plans were in solving the problem they identified. They use this information to decide what should be changed in objectives, strategies, and implementation tasks to assure even more success next time.

Evaluation issues. In Phase 5, teachers look at the following kinds of issues:

- **Were objectives achieved?** This is the primary criterion of success for the activity. Teachers review achievement, attitude, and observation data they have collected and decide if the technology-based method solved the problem(s) they had in mind. These data help them determine what should be changed to make the activity work better.

- **What do students say?** Some of the best suggestions on needed improvements come from students. Informal discussions with them yield a unique "consumer" focus on the activity.

- **Could improving instructional strategies improve results?** Technologies in themselves usually improve little; it is the way teachers use them that is critical. Look at the design of both the technology use and the learning activities surrounding it.

- **Could improving the environment improve results?** Sometimes a small change such as better scheduling or access to a printer can make a big difference in the success of the project.

- **Have I integrated technology well?** Use the Technology Impact Checklist (see Chapter 1, page 6 of this booklet) to determine if the activity has been "worth it."

Phase 5 questions. This phase in integrating technology requires answering two summary questions about evaluating and revising technology integration strategies. These questions are listed on the next page with suggestions for answering them in actual classroom situations:

1. **How well has the technology integration strategy worked?** To answer this question, review the collected data and use the checklist on page 6 of this booklet.

- **Achievement data:** If the problem was low student achievement, do data show students are achieving better than they were before? If the goal was improved motivation or attitudes, are they achieving at least as well as they did before? Is higher achievement consistent across the class, or did some students seem to profit more than others?

- **Attitude data:** If the problem was low motivation or students refusing to do required work, are there indications this behavior has improved? Has it improved for everyone or just for certain students?

- **Student comments:** Be sure to ask both lower-achieving and higher-achieving students for their opinions. Even if achievement and motivation seem to be improved, what do students say about how the activity went? Would they like to do similar activities again?

2. **What could be improved to make it work better?** Remember that the first time you do a technology-based activity, you can expect it will take longer and you will encounter more errors than in subsequent uses. The following areas are most often cited as needing improvement:

- **Scheduling:** If students request any change, it is usually for more time. This may or may not be feasible, but you can review the schedule to determine if additional time can be built in for learning software and/or for production work.

- **Technical skills:** It usually takes longer than expected for students to learn the new technology tools. How can this learning be expedited or supported better?

- **Efficiency:** The teacher complaint is usually that the activity took longer than expected to plan and carry out. Review the schedule to see if there is there any way this can be expedited.

The problem-based exercises in this chapter give you hands-on practice in applying Phase 5 of the TIP Model concepts you read in Chapter 1. Through scenario-based problem situations, you see how teachers go about evaluating and revising their technology integration strategy to maximize success and impact.

Scenarios to Read and Analyze – The following scenarios are continuations of the ones begun in Chapter 2. Answer the questions using information you have read about Phase 5 of the TIP Model in the Introduction to this chapter and in Chapter 1:

Scenario 1, Phase 5 – Mia and Lars were discussing her Internet-based multicultural project. "What do you think, Mia, was it worth all the work?" said Lars.

"Lars, just look at these pre-post data on the semantic differential," Mia said, clearly pleased with the results. "Nearly every student showed a major improvement in how they felt about people from the countries we were studying. It's hard to believe how much the e-mails and products affected how they look at other cultures. You've seen some of their products. I can't remember my students being so excited about something they've produced. Some booklets are more polished-looking than others, but they all show such insights and have such a wealth of information. Even I learned something from them. The web searches they did made a big difference."

Lars was impressed by the products, but still doubtful. "Yes, I can see these represent some real effort, and I'll admit I'm surprised by the quality, but how about what YOU had to do? Didn't it take a long time to get them up to speed on the technical skills? I remember you had some problems there?"

"Yes," admitted Mia, "It was touch-and-go there for awhile in the second week. When I talked to students about it, they told me what confused them and gave me some ideas on how I could do it better next time. You know my students; they aren't shy about telling me how I SHOULD have done it!

"One thing that became clear quickly," Mia continued, "was that production work is so time-consuming. I'm going to have to change the schedule somehow. I also have to make sure they know the deadlines are firm. They'd search and take digital photos forever, if I let them, and never get to do their products. We spent so much time on that, we didn't really have time to discuss their findings on comparisons of cultures."

"Well, I admit this captures my interest," said Lars. "But I can't help but wonder if their results would have been as good with just the e-mail exchanges and no time-consuming production work."

"Hmm, good question," said Mia.

S1.1 Although all Mia's groups did well on content overall, rubric scores revealed that most groups scored lower on one area: comparisons of cultural similarities and differences. What step could Mia add that may improve this outcome next time?

S1.2 Can you suggest a way of collecting data next time to answer Lars' question?

S1.3 If you found that only five of the seven groups were doing well on their final products, what might be one way to find out more about why this was happening?

S1.4 One teacher who observed the project told Mia it might be good to have the school district media/materials production office do the final work on the products for the students. Does this seem like a good idea? Why or why not?

Scenario 2, Phase 5 – Leroy was telling Arvella how his "aliens project" went. "I think I've created a monster," said Leroy, smiling, "but in a good way. My students are rabid to do more projects like this one. It became like a culture, with experts on various planets and even probe design specialists. And have you heard about the 'Alien Rescue Club' they've started?"

"Yes," said Arvella, grinning, "I've certainly heard about this project from other teachers. But what everyone wants to know is: did it improve their science skills?"

"I would have expected that this much excitement about a science activity had to have an impact on their inquiry skills, and I wasn't wrong," said Leroy. "They seemed to do better with each probe they designed and each set of data they got to analyze. Perhaps best of all, they started talking like scientists. Since the end of the project, nearly all of the students are using what I call 'inquiry-speak' when they do other work. I've even had some girls asking about careers in space exploration. I sent them to look at the NASA sites and the Space Camp sites on the Internet.

"Their problem solving checklists reflected good progress, too," Leroy continued. "Scores on the first ones they did were a little low, but the last ones were really fine in all groups. I only had two real problems. One was when some group members had to leave for special school events. That left a 'hole' in the group, and we had to improvise. Several students had to miss the last two days of the project for the band trip. The other problem was with getting access to computers. It would really have helped to have more computers right there in the room. I wish I had a five-computer workstation and printer like Amelia, the English teacher. That would make a big difference."

"How about their scores on the solar system test?" asked Arvella. "Were they better or worse, would you say?"

"That varied a lot," Leroy acknowledged. "I'm still trying to figure out why some students did so much better than others. Still, their attitudes toward science seem way up, and they are more on task than I've ever seen them. I think it was worth the 'controlled chaos' it created! Sometimes I felt like they were in charge of the classroom, and I was just a helpful assistant. It was a new feeling."

"Interesting," mused Arvella. "Maybe you should be 'just' a helpful assistant to them. Maybe that's the way it should be. What do you think?"

S2.1   Why do you think some of the students didn't do as well on the solar system test? Was there anything happening that could have affected their learning?

S2.2   Can you think of a way to improve results on the test for next time?

S2.3   How would you respond to Arvella's query? Is it okay for a teacher to be "just an assistant" in the classroom?

Phase 5 Problems to Analyze and Solve

P.1. Frank had his students do a one-week project using census data from the U. S. Census Bureau's GIS web site to answer questions about characteristics of their local area and do comparisons of growth patterns in various parts of the city. He wanted them to get a more active, hands-on role in exploring how population relates to civic issues. He had assigned four groups of eight students each, with each student in charge of a different part of the product. When he analyzed data from the project, he was encouraged with their progress over the concepts. He found that three of the four groups met criteria on their product. However, he overheard one of his students say they never wanted to do a project like this again.

P1.1 Would you say Frank's project was a success? Why or why not?

P1.2 How could he find out more about what the students did and didn't like about the project?

P1.3 Can you suggest any changes to the time frame and grouping strategies that may help him achieve better results?

P.2. From another language arts teacher, Verna heard about using *Inspiration*™ software to have students do concept maps before writing compositions. She always had trouble getting her lower-achieving sixth graders to create outlines before they started writing, and she thought doing concept maps might help. She showed them how to use the software and let them experiment with copying an example she had created. Then they did one of their own to prepare for a writing assignment. When she looked at what they had produced, most seemed to have thought through the ideas and were ready to do a well-structured composition. When she asked three of her better students how they liked the software, they expressed great delight with it and told her they wanted to use it again.

P2.1 Would you say Verna's technology use was a success? Why or why not?

P2.2 What performance data should she look at carefully to help her decide how successful it had been in addressing the problem?

P2.3 Is the interview data she gathered sufficient to get an accurate reading on how students liked the activity? Why or why not? What else might she do?

P.3. Geraldo wanted his students to do a project with multimedia software that would foster "habits of mind" such as solving problems and group cooperation in science learning, as well as improve their communication and writing skills. In week 1, he divided them into groups of three and had them use the Internet to locate a biome and answer questions about its characteristics. In week 2, he introduced a new multimedia software package to them and had them prepare presentations of their findings. By week 3 they were doing compositions to analyze and compare their findings across groups using a set of guidelines Geraldo gave them. However, they took a lot longer with their multimedia projects, and had only two days to complete their written compositions. Composition grades were very poor, and only three of the seven groups met criteria on the multimedia rubrics.

P3.1 Do Geraldo's findings indicate he should abandon this project or modify it? Explain.

P3.2 Why do you think they did so poorly on the multimedia projects?

P3.3 What change in his planning might improve the composition results?

P.4. Wilfred was a special education resource teacher who wanted to give students with dysgraphia (non-writing behavior) an alternative way to do homework and class assignments. He showed a couple of the students how to use a small portable "computer companion" with a keyboard and word processing program. They did their work wherever they were and downloaded it to a computer later and printed it out. Students quickly learned how to do the activity and were delighted with their new ability. For the first time, they turned in all assignments on time. However, on a brief survey he gave to the special education teachers, four of the five teachers indicated they would not use it for their own students with dysgraphia.

P4.1 Would you say findings indicate the project was a success? Why or why not?

P4.2 What should he do to find out why teachers responded in this way?

P4.3 What other data or information could he gather about the quality of students' written assignments that could help him decide how to improve the strategy?

P.5. Ivana had her tenth-grade health students use a nutrition simulation program to track their eating habits and weight gains/losses over the term. They worked in small groups to discuss, compare, and contrast data and write summary recommendations for each person on how to improve eating habits and weight. Data on the test and rubric showed that students' grasp of the subject was higher than ever before. However, data from the attitude survey showed that most girls disliked the work they did.

P5.1 Would you say findings indicate the project was a success? Why or why not?

P5.2 Why do you think the female students may have disliked this project?

P5.3 What could be changed to make the activity more successful?

PART I REVIEW EXERCISES
Introducing the Technology Integration Planning Model

Do **Exercises 1-5** on the Companion Website at: http://www.prenhall.com/roblyer. Click on the link for *Educational Technology in Action* Review Exercises, and use the links in each of the following sections to answer the review questions. Do **Exercise 6** by loading the Tutorials CD and using the files in the Part I Review Exercises Folder.

Exercise 1. Determining Relative Advantage

Teachers choose technology-based methods over other methods when they see the "relative advantage," i.e., the new method offers enough benefits to convince them to use it instead of the old one. Relative advantage is a perception or belief shaped by teachers' experience and by information they receive. One way teachers learn that a technology-based method has relative advantage is through reading research results. The Center for Applied Research in Educational Technology (CARET), a project of the International Society for Technology in Education (ISTE), summarizes "best evidence" research results on the impact of technology in education. Look at the results for the Student Learning area.

I.1 What are five questions CARET says teachers can ask to determine if technology-based methods have impact on student learning?
I.2 Describe two studies at the CARET web site that offer convincing evidence that a technology-based method has more impact on student learning than another method.

Exercise 2. Deciding on Objectives and Assessments

How should teachers decide on specific outcome objectives they want students to achieve? Most teachers look to more general outcome statements provided by state and/or district curriculum standards to help them derive specific student outcomes. Another source of curriculum outcomes is *Standards for Success*, a document created by the Association of American Universities (AAUU) to list competencies students should have before they enter college. When teachers need tools to assess curriculum outcomes, Kathy Schrock's Guide for Educators offers a variety of instruments teachers can use or modify.

I.3 Review the *Standards for Success* document and click on Standards for one of the content areas. Create an outcome statement based on one of these standards that you feel technology could help students achieve.
I.4 To assess the outcome, select an assessment instrument from Kathy Schrock's Guide for Educators web site. Modify it to match the outcome, if necessary.

Exercise 3. Designing Integration Strategies

Many excellent models of directed, constructivist, and combination strategies are available at the <u>Blue Web 'N</u> web site, a collection of links to outstanding online lessons.

I.5 Most "Web-based Tutorials" at the <u>Blue Web 'N</u> site use a directed approach. Select a tutorial under one of the content areas and state outcomes it is designed to achieve.

I.6 Most of the "Activities" at the <u>Blue Web 'N</u> site are based on constructivist approaches. Select one for a content area and state outcomes it is designed to achieve.

Exercise 4. Preparing the Instructional Environment

As teachers set up their classrooms for integrating technology, they must be aware of laws and regulations related to software and media. The <u>Software and Information Industry Association (SIIA)</u> has several summaries that can help answers teachers' questions about whether or not a planned use of software or media is legal under current rules. Also, teachers must be aware of district and/or school Internet usage policies (Acceptable Internet Use Policy or AUP) described in Warlick's article on the <u>Education World</u> site.

I.7 Read the <u>SIIA's</u> "*Is it OK for Schools to Copy Software?*" and answer this question: A science teacher has purchased a single copy of a simulation software package for the math/science department. She and the math teacher want to use it for an interdisciplinary project. She makes him a copy so that both will have it in their classrooms. Why is this permitted or not permitted under copyright law?

I.8 According to <u>Warlick's article</u>, what four things must every AUP contain? Why?

Exercise 5. Evaluating and Revising Instructional Strategies

Teachers can collect information in addition to achievement data to evaluate the impact of a technology-based integration strategy. Look at ideas for getting student feedback on this page at the <u>Indiana University web site</u>. Learn about <u>attitude instruments</u> or <u>interviews</u> you can design to assess the success of your integration strategy. Look at the <u>Fermiab Education Office</u> for an example classroom observation instrument and rubric.

I.9 Look at the *Technology Impact Checklist* on page 6 of this booklet. Create a <u>Likert scale</u> for this checklist with points for each "degree of agreement." Decide on a total score that would convince you that your technology-based strategy was successful.

I.10 Create 3-5 questions for a <u>structured interview</u> with your students to determine what aspects of your strategy need to be revised in order to improve them.

Exercise 6. Creating Classroom Products – Load the Tutorials CD that came with this book. Open the Adobe *Acrobat*® files for *Word* and *PowerPoint* tutorials, and create products as the tutorials direct. (Adobe's *Acrobat Reader*® is on the CD.)

Part II:
Using the TIP Model to Integrate Technology Resources

Chapter 7

Problem-based Exercises on Using the TIP Model for Instructional Software Integration

---

Introduction to Instructional Software Integration

Instructional software materials are programs created for the sole purpose of assisting teaching and learning in one of two ways: (1) delivering instruction using directed methods or (2) supporting learning using inquiry-based methods. Few software packages can be classified as a single category (e.g., a "tutorial package"). Each contains one or more of the following five software functions that help deliver or support instruction:

- **Drill and practice** – Presents items, prompts responses, gives feedback when students need multiple opportunities to work problems or practice for the purpose of committing information to memory. (Supports directed methods only)
- **Tutorial** – Acts like a human tutor by providing all information, guidance, and practice a student needs in order to learn a topic. (Supports directed methods only)
- **Simulation** – Models real or imaginary systems (e.g., genetic experiments, the government for a new fictional country) in order to help students learn the principles underlying the systems. (Supports directed or constructivist methods)
- **Instructional game** – Provides a drill or simulation with game-based rules and challenges. (Supports directed or constructivist methods)
- **Problem solving** – Either (1) teaches directly (through explanation and/or practice) the general approaches and steps involved in solving problems, or (2) helps students learn to solve problems in a given content area. (Supports directed or constructivist methods)

The following chart gives a brief summary of the instructional benefits and classroom applications of each of these five basic instructional software functions.

Instructional Software	Sample Instructional Benefits	Sample Classroom Uses
Drill and practice	<ul><li>Gives immediate feedback on correctness of answers</li><li>Increases motivation for students to practice</li><li>Saves teacher time on grading student work</li></ul>	<ul><li>Supplement or replace assigned worksheets and homework</li><li>Prepare students for tests</li></ul>

Instructional Software	Sample Instructional Benefits	Sample Classroom Uses
Tutorial	• Supplements or replaces teacher presentations • Presents instruction in more visual, self-paced, motivating way than teacher-delivered presentations	• Provides self-paced review of a topic after students have received classroom instruction • Supplies alternative way of learning when usual strategies do not work • Supplies instruction on topics for which teachers are not available
Simulation	• Compresses time or slows down processes so they can be studied • Makes demonstrations interactive • Allows safe experimentation • Allows simulated experiences that are not possible in real life • Saves money on consumable resources • Allows experiments to be repeated with variations • Makes situations controllable so they can be studied	• Replaces or supplements lab experiments, role playing, and field trips • Introduces new topics • Fosters exploration and process learning • Provides format that encourages cooperative group work
Instructional games	• Provides highly motivating format for practice	• Replaces worksheets and exercises • Provides format that encourages cooperative group work • Rewards good work
Problem solving	• Directed benefits: Focuses attention on required problem solving skills • Constructivist: Allows self-discovery of principles	• Allows concentrated practice of key problem solving skills • Fosters exploration and process learning • Provides format that encourages cooperative group work

Problem-based exercises in this chapter give you hands-on practice in matching software functions to instructional needs and integrating software into instructional environments. Through scenario-based problem situations, you can see how teachers go about selecting and using instructional software.

Scenarios to Read and Analyze – The following scenarios are examples of integrating instructional software. After reading Chapter 4 in *Integrating Educational Technology into Teaching* (2003), answer the questions about using the TIP Model to integrate these strategies effectively:

Scenario 1, Software – Based on a lesson idea in: "Breeding Mice the Easy Way" by Randy Bell, Emily Yam, and Lynn Bell. *Learning and Leading with Technology*, 2003, Vol. 30, Number 7, pp. 22-27.

Elton, a high school biology teacher, was talking with Qing, a colleague from another school. "Do you ever get frustrated when you teach your kids Mengelian genetics principles?" asked Elton. "It's such exciting stuff to me, yet I can't get them interested. I guess there's just such a disconnect between the actual breeding results that display principles and how I can show it to them. Most of them just don't get it."

"Actually, I have been using something pretty exciting," said Qing. "There is a software I heard about at a workshop last fall and had a chance to play with after the demo. It has an excellent tutorial sequence in the introduction and a simulation that lets students do hands-on experiments to explore dominant and recessive traits. It's called *Mouse Genetics*, and it's available online at http://www.explorescience.com".

"Really?" said Elton. "How do you use it in your classroom?"

"I start off with a whole-class discussion, asking them how they think dog and cat breeders get the physical features they want. Then we go through the tutorial with a big-screen monitor on my classroom computer; the kids really get involved because the presentation is so interactive and visual. I just have to keep my better students from shouting out all the answers. Then I break them into groups and pose a simple question about offspring they expect in a certain situation. They go into the "Virtual Mouse House" and do the simulation to answer the question. It takes off from there. They get good experience creating explanations for unexpected results, and that leads naturally into deriving Mendel's Laws. For a final project, I have each group do a *PowerPoint* presentation of a law with examples. It's pretty neat."

"I'll say!" said Elton enthusiastically. "Can I use your handouts, do you think?"

S1.1 What problem did these biology teachers have and in what ways did the software provide a good solution? What is the relative advantage of the new method?

S1.2 Is the method Qing describes directed, inquiry-based, or a combination? Explain.

S1.3 How can Qing structure the demo activity to keep his better students from dominating it and keep the other students from participating? How would it change the activity if Elton has only one computer in his class?

S1.4 What outcomes would Elton and Qing want to assess? What measures could they use to assess them?

Scenario 2, Software –Based on a lesson idea in: "Do you think you might be wrong? Confirmation bias in problem solving" by J. Johnson. *Arithmetic Teacher*, 1987, Vol. 34, No. 9, pp. 13-16.

"Middle school students think they know everything, don't they?" Farley, the eighth-grade math teacher remarked to his colleague Vidalia. "I think that could be one of culprits responsible for their high error rate on math word problems in some of the standardized tests. They jump to conclusions and don't bother to test them out once they think they've got the answer. I wish I could get them to stop that behavior."

"I agree completely," said Vidalia, "and I have a software package that I use to help them see that very problem and use a systematic approach to getting correct answers. It's called *King's Rule®*, and it lets them generate and test hypotheses in math. It has a 'Hidden Rules Game' my students just love; I think it changes how they look at solving problems."

"Wow!" Farley exclaimed. "How does it work?"

"Let's say the software presents the number sequence 16-18-20. I ask the students to give me the rule and another example of it. Invariably, my class smart-aleck will say 'Oh, that's stupid. It's just counting by two's!' I say 'Okay, let's put in an example, and they say something like '4-6-8.' It's correct, of course, but it's not the right answer. I say, 'Does anyone else have another idea?' They know something's up and, with a little coaching, I get them to try something like 4-8-12, and it says it's correct. That flabbergasts them; it also draws them in. They start proposing alternatives like 'ascending numbers,' so I ask 'How would you eliminate that rule?"

"After the demo," continued Vidalia, "They are rabid to use the software. But first I give them a set of rules THEY have to abide by as they work in small groups: (1) First, list all rules that could apply. (2) Test each one by coming up with a way to eliminate it. (3) State the rule on a paper handout I give them. I tell them they have to start with the 'Easy' level and proceed to harder ones, and also that they have to give everyone a turn and leave out no one in the group."

"Wow, this is great!" said Farley. "Do you have a way of testing how well they can do this and whether this ability actually transfers to word problems?"

"The software has a built-in quiz they can take, said Vidalia nodding, "Then I give them a paper quiz. I haven't really checked for transfer yet. Any suggestions?"

S2.1 What problems did the teachers have? How did software provide good solutions? What software functions are used? (NOTE: Names aren't always accurate!)

S2.2 How could Farley find out if students' skills transferred to other math problems?

S2.3 If the teachers needed more than one copy of the software for the small-group work, what would they need to do to provide this?

S2.4 When Farley tried the activity, he found that 24 of his 30 students could pass the quiz. What could he do to find out why some students still had problems?

Instructional Software Integration Problems to Analyze and Solve

P.1. Andie uses a program called *Spelling Bee* to give her students practice before a spelling test or the language arts part of a standardized test. She knows the secret to her students' doing well in spelling is getting them to spend time on thinking about the words; she finds she can get them to spend more time with helpful practicing than she would with any paper-pencil exercise or other format. The software presents words via audio prompt and lets students enter correct spellings. They get points for every correct answer. If they play alone and attain a score they are shooting for, they win the spelling bee. They can also compete against each other in pairs.

P1.1 What software function is Andie using? What did it offer that made it a good match for the problem?

P1.2 If Andie wanted to have students practice in pairs to compete against each other, how would she have to do this to make sure some students wouldn't become too frustrated by losing all the time?

P1.3 Since the software gives audio prompts and feedback, what would Andie have to do if she wanted to use this effectively in a classroom of 30 students?

P.2. Sydney's students were not interested in learning about the U. S. Constitution. She wants to show them it is a document that affects their lives every day and in many situations they or people they know might encounter. Rather than just telling them about it, she found a software package that lets them practice applying it. They role-play various people faced with creating articles of confederation that would let them deal effectively with issues such as: threats to their borders, needs for currency, trade disputes, internal disagreements about key issues, and separate rights for states vs. central power. As they work in groups on various problems, they come to understand why laws are necessary and how they affect our lives. As a final activity, each group presents an article of confederation and illustrates how it works in practice.

P2.1 What software function is Sydney using? What did it offer that made it a good match for the problem?

P2.2 What outcomes would you want to assess after this activity? How would you state these outcomes?

P2.3 How would you measure students' progress on these outcomes?

P.3. In her Spanish I class, Sharon is having her students write an e-mail newsletter describing in Spanish their school and events in their community to students in a Puerto Rico classroom. She finds that her students' Spanish vocabulary is very limited, and she wants to give them practice in using Spanish equivalents for many English words. She locates a software package that provides vocabulary practice by presenting words in English or Spanish to which they must supply equivalents in the opposite language. If they supply the correct word, the program pronounces both words. The Teacher Manual gives a list of all the words.

P3.1 What kind of software function does this software provide and why does Sharon think the students need it?

P3.2 Would it be best for students to use this package individually, in small groups, or as a whole class?

P3.3 How would you assess whether this program was helping students learn enough vocabulary?

P.4. Carson finds that students in his honors algebra class can solve algebra equations, but they can't identify situations in everyday life that require them to set up and solve a simple equation. He finds a software package that has "virtual stores" in which students must solve various problems in order to "buy" items. They must use algebra equations to solve these problems. Carson has his students work in small groups to practice solving the problems and stating strategies they used.

P4.1 What kind of software function does this software provide and why does Carson think the students need it?

P4.2 What outcomes should Carson expect and how should he state them?

P4.3 What would be the best ways to assess these outcomes?

P.5. Wanda's science class is an academically diverse group, with some students learning concepts very quickly and others needing much more time to review and work on them. She has found a software series that provides a complete teaching sequence (instruction, practice items, testing) on each topic in the middle school physical sciences. Some students use it for review of topics they find particularly difficult. Others use it to "catch up" when they have been absent. However, the faster students also use it to jump ahead and learn advanced topics on their own.

P5.1 What kind of software function does this software provide and what problem does Wanda have that it addresses?

P5.2 Would one copy of the software meet Wanda's needs? Why or why not?

P5.3 How could Wanda find out if most students like using the software?

Chapter 8

Problem-based Exercises on Using the TIP Model for Software Tool Integration

Introduction to Software Tool Integration

Software tools are programs created for the purpose of helping people accomplish various tasks. For example, word processing software helps people produce and format typed text, and graphics software tools help them produce and format images. Most software tools were originally designed for use in the workplace, rather than the school. Though most were not created specifically for education, they have become useful resources for teachers and students because each supplies one or more of these benefits:

- **Makes work more efficient** – Most software tools make it easier and faster to create written or digital products and to revise and update them once they are created. Using these tools can motivate students to do activities they would not otherwise attempt.
- **Improves appearance of products** – By using software tools, teachers and students no longer need to rely on expensive professionals to produce polished-looking products such as newsletters or certificates. Users of software tools are limited only by their own creativity and design skills.
- **Improves information accuracy** – Some software tools make it easier to do calculations and keep more accurate records. They also make it easier to spot and correct content errors.
- **Supports interaction and sharing** – Since software tools can do the manual labor involved in creating products and can support research and information-gathering, they make it easier for groups to work together on projects. Also, putting products in a digital format makes it easier to share them on a disk or via e-mail.

The following chart gives a brief summary of the instructional software tools and sample classroom applications of each. Read more about these tools and their uses in Chapters 5-6 of *Integrating Educational Technology into Teaching* (Roblyer, 2003).

Sample Software Tools	Sample Classroom Uses
Word processing	Teacher letters, flyers, and other documents; student writing processes; dynamic group products; language exercises
Spreadsheets	Demonstrations of math principles; student tables and charts; support for math problem solving; asking "what if?" questions; data storage and analysis; projecting grades

Databases	Teacher resource inventories; personalized letters; ready access to student information; support for teaching research and study skills, organization skills, posing and testing hypotheses, searching for information during research
Desktop publishing software	Working individually or in small groups, students create their own letterhead, brochures, flyers/posters, newsletters, books
Test generators/test item banks	Teachers can create test item banks and generate various versions of tests from them. Can administer tests online.
Worksheet /puzzle generators	Teachers produce exercises for student skill practice
IEP generators	Teachers create Individual Educational Plans (IEP's) for special education students
Certificate makers	Teachers and students create awards and recognitions
Form makers	Teachers create forms to gather data from students, others
Gradebooks	Teachers keep track of and calculate students grades
Statistical packages	Teachers and students analyze data from experiments and research projects
CMI and testing tools	Teachers keep track of student and class progress on required curriculum objectives; use data to support decision-making
Image processing tools	Teachers and students use to illustrate documents, web pages
Charting/graphing tools	Students use to create charts and graphs to illustrate and study data summaries
Clip art, video, and sound collections	Teachers and students insert these into documents and media they create
Video development tools	Teachers can create video demonstrations; students create videos to illustrate principles they have learned
Outliners	Help students organize their ideas to prepare for writing
Concept mapping software	Students use these to help organize their ideas visually in preparation for writing and to show how sub-concepts that make up a topic area are related to each other
Scheduling software	Helps teachers organize their time and plan activities
Electronic encyclopedias, atlases, and dictionaries	Help students research topics they have been assigned
CAD systems	Helps students create visual models of houses and other structures as they study design concepts
Music editors	Help students create and revise their own musical pieces
MBLs/CBLs	Help students collect and analyze data from experiments
GPS and GIS systems	Help students study geographical information and concepts

Problem-based exercises in this chapter give you hands-on practice in matching software functions to instructional needs and integrating software into instructional environments. Through scenario-based problem situations, you can see how teachers go about selecting and using software tools.

Scenarios to Read and Analyze – The following scenarios are examples of integrating software tools into curriculum lessons. After reading Chapters 5-6 in *Integrating Educational Technology into Teaching* (Roblyer, 2003), answer the questions about using the TIP Model to integrate these strategies effectively:

Scenario 1, Software Tools – Based on a lesson idea in: "Desktop Poetry Project" by Emily Scharf and Judith Cramer. *Learning and Leading with Technology,* 2002, Vol. 29, N0. 6, pp. 28-31, 50-51.

Mort and Chloe, two middle school language arts teachers, were talking in the teachers lounge. "You know what a pain it is to put together the annual eighth-grade literary magazine," said Chloe. "We spend all those hours and hours of typing and editing, then have to format it for the print shop to work with? Well, I think I've found a way to cut all the trouble in half and let ALL the students participate in the publication instead of just a selected few."

"This I've got to hear," said Mort. "I'm the one who usually gets the job of telling students they weren't selected for the magazine. It would be so much better if they all knew their work would appear. I think it would really motivate them to do their best in class."

"Yes, that's what I have been thinking," agreed Chloe. "If my plan works, I think it would keep every student's interest in the language arts class they take the semester before they graduate; you know, the one where they have to study all the poetry forms?"

"Okay, now I'm really interested," laughed Mort. "What is this strategy? Magic?"

Chloe smiled. "Sort of. I guess you could call it 'desktop publishing magic.' Our technology resource teacher, Fiona, and I came up with the idea of students creating an eighth-grade student poetry anthology. Every student would study the poetry forms and present their favorite ones in class, as they usually do. But then they begin work on their anthology contributions. If they all do their poems in Microsoft *Word*®, we can put the files on our school server, which would make them easy to download and work on. Then the students can help create style sheets in Adobe *PageMaker*® for each section of the anthology. By selecting typefaces and creating page designs, it will help them learn more about how poems often communicate meaning by the ways they appear on the page."

"This sounds so neat!" exclaimed Mort. "Count me in!"

"There's plenty to do," said Chloe, reaching for a pen. "Can I put you down for creating assessment strategies to evaluate and grade students' work?"

1.1 What problems did these teachers have and in what ways did the software project provide a good solution? What is the relative advantage of doing the anthology?

1.2 Is this project directed, inquiry-based, or a combination? Explain.

1.3 How would you recommend arranging the desktop publishing software so that all 70 eighth-grade students could help with the design tasks??

1.4 What outcomes need to be assessed? How would you recommend they be assessed?

Scenario 2, Software Tools – Based on a lesson idea in: "Geography is Everywhere: Connecting Schools and Communities with GIS" by Marsha Alibrandi. *Learning and Leading with Technology,* 2002, Vol. 29, No. 7, pp. 32-37.

"Why so glum, Keisha?" said Ernie, sitting down beside the social studies teacher in the lunchroom.

"I'm not really glum, Ernie," said Keisha. "I guess I'm just thinking about how I can do a project I want to do. You've heard about Global Information Systems, a.k.a, GIS, haven't you? In the workshop I went to last summer, they said GIS tools are going to become as essential to studying geography and local issues as word processing is to learning to write. I'd always like my students to learn the most up-to-date tools so I try to teach them to use what the professionals use in their workplaces. I know of some local GIS sources, but I'm trying to figure out a meaningful project they can do with GIS data."

"Maybe I can suggest something," said Ernie. "You know my class does the environmental studies project every fall in the Little River area. They collect water samples and do tests to analyze sources of degradation and contaminants. Then they try to determine the sources of these withdrawals and contaminants. It would be great to have GIS information to help students with these analyses."

"Wow, this could be so powerful!" said Keisha thoughtfully. "Maybe our classes could work together in the fall. I could teach my Current Social Issues class how to use the systems, and then they could help your students create a database of their findings linked to GIS data from the town planning office. I know they would help me out with this."

"How about if I could get our local school partner Allied Industries to donate some handheld Global Positioning Systems for my students to use as they collect data? Wouldn't that help identify the locations for our database?"

"Sure, that would be great!" said Keisha, nodding. "The two would work together well, and it would make it clearer to all the students how GIS data are used in the GPS's they see in their cars. This sounds like a winner to me!"

"It also sounds like a lot of work for us," said Ernie, grinning. "Most of my good ideas seem to mean more work for me. I guess we need to get started, huh?"

S2.1 What instructional problems did Keisha see that she wanted to address in a new project? In what ways were GIS's such a good solution to the problem(s)?

S2.2 What work was Ernie referring to that they would have to do? In which phase(s) of the TIP Model would this work occur?

S2.3 If you were purchasing the handheld GPS's for 35 students to use, how many would you request that the school's company partner donate?

S2.4 What outcomes would need to be assessed in each class (Current Issues and Environmental Science) and how would you recommend they be assessed?

Software Tool Integration Problems to Analyze and Solve

P.1. Gilbert wanted to demonstrate various principles of probability to his junior high advanced math students and then let them test hypotheses on data sets to show the principles in action. However, the exercises he had them do required a series of calculations on a set of numbers. It took the students a long time to do these calculations with a calculator because they had to keep re-entering the numbers and made a lot of entry errors. All the time spent on entering figures and correcting errors made it difficult for them to focus on the hypothesis testing.

P1.1 What software tool would you recommend Gilbert use to address this problem?
P1.2 What would be the relative advantage of using this software tool?
P1.3 Would it be better to have the students work individually or in groups to do the exercises? How would you arrange the computer systems to carry out this strategy?

P.2. Chinita was teaching her students higher-level study skills. She wanted to show them how they could outline a complicated article by drawing a diagram to illustrate the ideas in it and how they relate to each other. She found this visual display worked very well for her, and she wanted her students to learn it, too. However, she found the approach didn't work very well because students who were just learning this technique tended to make a lot of mistakes drawing the boxes and connecting lines, and then they didn't want to do the work of erasing and revising them.

P2.1 What software tool would you recommend Chinita use to address this problem?
P2.2 What would be the relative advantage of using this software tool?
P2.3 Would this kind of activity be best done on an individual basis, in pairs, or in groups? Explain why.

P.3. Whenever Jackie had her students do a research project for her social studies class, she would send them to the library/media center to look up the information in reference books. Since several students usually wanted to use the same text, there was a lot of wasted time; it was difficult to keep students focused on the information-gathering. Jackie had heard about a software tool that several students could use easily at the time same and had pictures and videos, as well as text descriptions, so students got more out of the information they did find.

P3.1 What software tool does Jackie have in mind to address this problem?
P3.2 What would be the relative advantage of using this software tool?
P3.3 How would it be possible for a class of 30 students to use this tool at the same time?

P.4. Hortense's Consumer Math classes have over 40 students each. She likes to give them weekly quizzes to make sure everyone is keeping up on the skills and spot students who may need additional help. However, the class is so large and students sit so close together, she also feels she needs several different versions of each test to prevent "sharing answers." She has heard about a software tool that she can use to create a pool of items and that lets her generate different versions of the same test from the items.

P4.1 What software tool would you recommend Hortense use to address this problem?
P4.2 What would be the relative advantage of using this software tool?
P4.3 If she wanted the versions to be very different from each other, what would she have to do to make this tool work well for her purposes?

P.5. Charlene wants to make her middle school classes hands-on, with students doing experiments by collecting and analyzing their own data. However, taking accurate readings of variables such as temperature is very difficult for her students to do. Also, the students find the repetitious recording and calculating very boring, and it is difficult to keep them focused on the experiment. She has heard about a software tool that can collect temperature readings quickly and feed the data automatically into a computer for analysis. She thinks that using this tool will be much more motivating to her students than doing all the operations by hand.

P5.1 What software tool would you recommend Charlene use to address this problem?
P5.2 What would be the relative advantage of using this software tool?
P5.3 If Charlene has 36 students in a class and only 5 such tools, how could she arrange the tool so that all students could learn to use it?

Chapter 9

Problem-based Exercises on Using the TIP Model for Multimedia/Hypermedia Integration

Introduction to Multimedia and Hypermedia Integration

Newspapers, radio, and television are media that allow various forms of communication in our society. Education, too, has its media to allow teachers and students to communicate information in various ways. Increasing use of multimedia/hypermedia tools in education reflects our growing cultural reliance on interactive modes of communication. Although books and other static text materials remain important information sources, students expect to experience pictures, video, animation, and sound in the classroom, just as they do outside it.

Many changes have taken place in the world of multimedia in recent years. Materials such as Microsoft *PowerPoint®* that were once just a sequence of text-and-image slides have gradually added sound, video, and other features. Also, many of today's most popular products developed with presentation or video software are now displayed on the Internet. It is for these reasons that the words "multimedia" (i.e., many media) and "hypermedia" (i.e., interconnected media) have come to be used interchangeably. (See multimedia tools to develop and display web pages for the Internet described in the next chapter.) The following are some of the benefits multimedia/hypermedia materials bring to education:

- **Variety of channels for communicating information** – Supplementing text-based information with pictures, video, and sound captures students' attention; using multiple channels makes it more likely they will understand and remember concepts.
- **Interactive qualities** – Multimedia materials that require student input and offer immediate feedback help keep them involved in the learning activity.
- **Flexibility for demonstrating learning** – In line with Gardner's Multiple Intelligences Theory, multimedia allow students more than one way to show what they have learned.
- **Support for practicing creativity, critical thinking, and information organization** – When students create their own multimedia products, they have opportunities to think creatively and critically about how best to communicate and organize information.
- **Support for cooperative group work** – Multimedia production also gives students a motivating format for learning skills required for working cooperatively in groups.

The following chart gives a brief summary of the types of multimedia/hypermedia sample classroom applications of each. Read more about these materials and their uses in Chapter 7 of *Integrating Educational Technology into Teaching* (Roblyer, 2003).

Types of Multimedia/Hypermedia	Sample Classroom Uses of Multimedia/Hypermedia
Commercial multimedia/hypermedia packages: Interactive instructional software	Use for the same classroom applications as instructional software (See Chapter 7 in this book.)
Interactive storybooks	Use to supplement or replace children's traditional book reading to promote reading comprehension and encourage critical thinking about story structure
Reference materials (electronic encyclopedias, atlases, dictionaries)	Support student research and information-gathering for individual and group reports and projects
Interactive videodisc systems	Although interactive CD and DVD formats have superceded videodisc ones, many schools still use videodiscs for demonstrations to introduce topics, illustrate concepts, and make learning more visual, especially in history and science topics.
Multimedia/hypermedia authoring systems: Presentation software (e.g., Microsoft *PowerPoint*®)	Use for teacher presentations and demonstrations; and student book reports, project reports, presentations, and personal portfolios
Video production/editing (e.g., *iMovie*®, *Adobe Premiere*®)	Use to teach visual communication methods and for student project presentations, newscasts, dramatizations, and video clips for a web page
Hypermedia software (e.g., *HyperStudio*®, and *Macromedia Director*®)	Use for teacher presentations and demonstrations; and student book reports, project reports, presentations, and personal portfolios

Problem-based exercises in this chapter give you hands-on practice in integrating multimedia/hypermedia uses into instructional environments. Through scenario-based problem situations, you can see how teachers go about using multimedia/hypermedia tools of various kinds to support and enhance learning.

Scenarios to Read and Analyze – The following scenarios are examples of integrating multimedia/hypermedia tools into curriculum lessons. After reading Chapter 7 in *Integrating Educational Technology into Teaching* (Roblyer, 2003), answer the questions about using the TIP Model to integrate these strategies effectively:

Scenario 1, Multimedia/Hypermedia – Based on a lesson idea in: "Reading and Writing the Digital Way: Using Digital Books to Teach Math" by Trena L. Wilkerson. *Learning and Leading with Technology,* 2001, Vol. 29, Number 3, pp. 42-45, 60-61.

Lavinia, the math resource teacher for the Premier Elementary School, was listening to Edwardo and Wilma, two of the school's second-grade teachers.

"You know," said Edwardo, "I'm really tired of seeing so many of my students mentally 'drop out' of my math lessons at such a young age. Math concepts are so relevant to their lives, not to mention their success in school; but as hard as I try, I can't get some of them in touch with the whole idea of thinking mathematically. They just don't get it."

"I feel the same way," agreed Wilma. "My students like manipulatives and games, but there is only so much you can do with them. I keep thinking we need to make our math strategies more exciting and engaging. Kids spend hours on those computer games, but we can't get them to focus for 30 minutes on math ideas."

"You know," said Lavinia, "I saw something at the math magnet school last week that might be the answer you're looking for. They use *PowerPoint*® and *HyperStudio*® to create what they called 'digital books' to illustrate math principles like whole-number operations, number sets, patterns, and geometric shapes. It didn't take teachers long to create them, and they seemed to have great fun at it. During class, they projected each book on a big screen so students could go up and touch things as the class discussed it; they even had an audio feature to read it aloud if students wanted to use it after the demonstration.

"After the lesson," continued Lavinia, "students got to create their own digital book pages to show what they learned, so it became an assessment activity. The teachers had a template set up, so it was easy for their students to insert clip art and draw lines to represent math ideas. The teachers say they have never seen kids so excited about doing math!"

"This sounds so neat," exclaimed Edwardo. "Can I visit the school and see how they do it?" "Me, too," said Wilma. "When do we start?"

1.1   What problems did the teachers have for which Lavinia felt a digital book strategy provided a good solution? What is the relative advantage of doing such an activity?

1.2   Is this project directed, inquiry-based, or a combination? Explain.

1.3   What equipment and software would you need to obtain to carry out such lessons and how many of each would you need?

1.4   How would you assess whether or not students' attitudes about math had changed as a result of this strategy?

Scenario 2, Multimedia/Hypermedia – Based on a lesson idea in: "Digital Video Goes to School" by Helen Hoffenberg and Marianne Handler. *Learning and Leading with Technology,* 2001, Vol. 29, No. 2, pp. 10-15.

The high school's faculty meeting was just breaking up and teachers were gathering their belongings and walking out, talking and laughing on their way down the hall. "Hey, Latifah," said Phil, the history teacher, walking up to the school principal, "Do you have a minute? I have this idea I want to run by you."

"Uh-oh," laughed Latifah, "Another of your ideas! What's your brainstorm, Phil?"

"Well," said Phil, "You know how excited students get about doing the video news and weather announcements each morning? The Technology Class members are the only ones who get to do them, but they have such a great time taping and interviewing and creating funny scripts. Sometimes I hear students in my classes talking about the morning videos, so they really seem to capture their attention. I've been thinking I want to give more students opportunities to do video production projects. I was talking to a friend of mine at Topnotch High School, and she says they have their students do video projects in nearly every content area. They find it helps keep students more involved in the content and gives them practice in organizing ideas, talking to people – even in reading and writing. The teachers put some of the videos on their school Web server so they can show them to friends and parents."

"It does sound interesting," said Latifah. "Is this something you that would work just for your history classes, Phil, or would other teachers here be interested in doing it?"

"Actually," said Phil, "I've already talked to several other teachers and we've brainstormed what I think are some good ideas. Luther in Physical Education and Stella in Physics had this idea for working together to have students create video demonstrations of physics principles in sports. I'd love to get my students interviewing local history experts and creating historical videos. Tim in Biology thought we might combine my project with his unit on local ecologies. Phyllis in Technology Education said she'd teach us how to use digital video cameras and storyboard the scripts for the final products. What do you think?"

Latifah smiled. "I think you're about to ask me for some money," she said. "Yes?"

"Actually," said Phil, "All we would need is a couple more digital cameras, and I've found an incredible price on this web site that gives discounts for educators. A real steal!"

S2.1 What instructional problems did Phil see that he wanted to address with video-based projects? What did he feel was the relative advantage of this strategy?

S2.2 What other planning tasks would be necessary for teachers to carry out in preparation for projects like this (e.g., students' skills involved in interviewing, taping).

S2.3 Pick any of the projects Phil describes and list some of the outcomes that would need to be assessed. What would be good ways to assess them?

S2.4 Can you think of any privacy and legal issues that teachers would have to address so students could take video of local people and places?

Multimedia/Hypermedia Integration Problems to Analyze and Solve

P.1. Joaquin is looking for a more motivating alternative to traditional written book reports. His fifth-grade students don't especially like reading books or writing book reports. Joaquin was talking to a colleague who uses *HyperStudio®* multimedia software to make doing book reports more appealing to students.

P1.1 Describe how you think using *HyperStudio®* multimedia software would make it more likely Joaquin's students would enjoy doing book reports.

P1.2 What would be the relative advantage of using this software tool?

P1.3 Would it be better to have the students work individually or in groups to do the exercises? How would you arrange the computer systems to carry out this strategy?

P.2. Clint and Sandy, two junior high school social studies teachers, plan a school-wide project to document the history of the local area by focusing on the families whose personal histories are intertwined with the history of the region. They plan to have students interview many individual family members and research local sources of historical information. Then they want the students to organize all the information into a book about the history of the local region.

P2.1 What multimedia tools could Clint and Sandy use to enhance and support this project?

P2.2 What would be the relative advantage of using such multimedia tools?

P2.3 This kind of project would require a lot of work to research and organize information and to produce the final product. Suggest some ways this work could be divided up and accomplished among classes to model for students how to organize work tasks in a large, complex project.

P.3. Eli is a fourth-grade teacher who has several students in his class who speak English as a second language. He works on increasing the comprehension skills for each of his students and encourages them to read books and stories to practice their skills. His students who speak English as their second language have trouble reading independently, and Eli does not have the time to read to each of them individually. He would like a way they can have books read aloud to them in an enjoyable way and also answer comprehension questions about what they have heard and read.

P3.1 What software tool could help Eli address this problem?

P3.2 What would be the relative advantages of using this software tool with his students who speak English as a second language?

P3.3 How would it be possible for these students to use this tool in class but not disturb or distract other students?

P.4. Elinor is a high school curriculum coordinator who wants the students to prepare an electronic portfolio they can take with them to display the quality of their work and what they have accomplished throughout their courses. She would like this to include film footage of them giving class presentations, as well as digital samples of their work. The completed portfolio for graduating seniors would be placed on a CD they could take with them.

P4.1 What software tool would you recommend Elinor use to address this problem?

P4.2 What would be the relative advantage of using this software tool?

P4.3 If she wanted teachers to assist with this activity, what would she have to make sure was done before the portfolio concept was introduced to students?

P.5. Belinda's eighth-grade language arts students have a spelling test every Friday, and spelling counts for 10% of their overall semester grade. There is no time during the regular class period during the week to allow students to practice, and it is obvious from their grades that many students do not study the words outside class. Belinda thought of a way to use Microsoft *PowerPoint*® software to make sure her students see all the spelling words and hear them pronounced every time they come in the classroom and every time they leave.

P5.1 How do you think Belinda uses *PowerPoint*® software to address this problem?

P5.2 What would be the relative advantage of using *PowerPoint*® software for this purpose?

P5.3 Which of *PowerPoint*®'s multimedia benefits is Belinda using for this activity?

Chapter 10

Problem-based Exercises on Using the TIP Model for Integrating the Internet and Other Distance Resources into the Curriculum

---

Introduction to Integrating the Internet and Other Distance Resources

The Internet and its related resources (e.g., e-mail, instant messaging, listservs) have become such fixtures of modern life that it is difficult to remember when we didn't rely on them. It makes sense that resources that permeate so many activities in our society should also be integrated into students' learning experiences. The following are some of the most important benefits the Internet and its related materials bring to education:

- **Easy and rapid communication** – Through e-mail and web pages, students, teachers, and parents can more easily exchange and keep each other updated on important information.
- **Access to expert resources and information not locally available** – Each local community has information resources (e.g., libraries), expert resources (e.g., professionals such as police and doctors), and information-rich locations (e.g., local factories, museums) that students can use as experts sources when they study various topics. The Internet expands these expert resources to include people, sites, and locations all over the world.
- **Access to up-to-date information** – News, weather, and other web sites provide students with up-to-the-minute information and data sources for use in projects and lessons.
- **Easy sharing of information and work products** – The capability to exchange notes, e-mail files, and view information on web pages supports students as they work on projects with each other and with teachers.
- **Support for cooperative group work** – Web research and web site production gives students motivating formats to learn skills required for working cooperatively in groups.
- **Support for learning information and visual literacy skills** – Evaluating and designing web pages is a useful, motivational way to teach skills students will need to be savvy consumers and developers of visual and text information.

The following chart gives a brief summary of some the types of Internet and distance learning resources and sample teaching and learning applications of each. Read more about these materials and their integration strategies in Chapter 8 of *Integrating Educational Technology into Teaching* (Roblyer, 2003).

Types of Internet Resources	Sample Classroom Applications of Internet Resources
Web browsers	Virtual field trip projects; self-instructional tutorials; support for classroom communications among students, teachers, and parents; webquest projects to solve problems or locate information; social action projects; web-based scavenger hunts
Search engines	Online research on assigned topics and projects, locating contact information for experts
E-mail and listservs	Keypal projects, telementoring activities
Chatrooms and instant messaging	Support for project work among students and teachers working together on projects at a distance
Web page development resources	Students' development of web pages and sites to display work products

Problem-based exercises in this chapter give you hands-on practice in integrating the Internet and other distance resources into instructional environments. Through scenario-based problem situations, you can see how teachers go about selecting and using these tools to support teaching and learning.

Scenarios to Read and Analyze – The following scenarios are examples of integrating the Internet and other distance resources into curriculum lessons. After reading Chapter 8 in *Integrating Educational Technology into Teaching* (Roblyer, 2003), answer the questions about using the TIP Model to integrate these strategies effectively:

Scenario 1, Internet – Based on a lesson idea in: "Virtual Art" by Glen Bull and Gina Bull. *Learning and Leading with Technology*, 2001, Vol. 29, No. 3, pp. 54-58.

Gertrude, local sculptor and artist and mother of two elementary school children, was talking with her daughter's teacher, Cecily.

"I despair, Cecily, I just really despair of getting our kids exposed to high-quality art in this backwater," said Gertrude, waving her hands dismissively in the general direction of the small, rural town where they lived. "Of course, I take my girls to the city whenever I can, and there is always my illustrated art book collection. But, really, my dear, no art museums close enough for our children to visit? It's an educational tragedy!"

Cecily smiled. "Yes, I agree it does present a challenge. We want all our students to be artistically literate, as well as read-and-writing literate, don't we? I think you'll be interested in one of the projects I'm doing this year. Next month we're taking a virtual field trip to major art exhibits around the world. I've already identified some of the web sites. Most of the major art institutes and museums have extensive web collections, you know.

"Look at this site the Chicago Art Institute just put up to show its collection of Iraqi art objects from 2500 B.C.," she continued, walking over to her classroom computer. "We can't get to Chicago, of course, and the exhibit will be there only a short time anyway, but the web site will be up for the rest of the year or longer." She clicked on the bookmarked web site and displayed some of the objects. Gertrude's eyes grew wider with each page she saw.

"This is remarkable!" Gertrude exclaimed. "I wanted to see this exhibit myself, but I just can't get away this time of year."

"Yes," said Cecily, "This is one of about a dozen museum sites we'll see. In a way, it's better than going to them in person; we can see more items faster this way. The kids will have a list of items to find and questions to answer about the paintings, sculptures, and other objects they see. Then they'll do their own art based on ideas they get from the museums. Finally, we'll make a web site collection of their work and put it on the school server."

"My dear, this is sensational!" cried Gertrude. "Perhaps there is hope for our children's art education after all! I hope you'll let me help with this."

S1.1   What problems did Cecily and Gertrude see that the Internet project could help with? What are the relative advantages of doing a virtual field trip as opposed to a real one?

S1.2   Is this project directed, inquiry-based, or a combination? Explain.

S1.3   What materials would Cecily have to prepare before she began this project?

S1.4   How might Cecily introduce this project to the students? How might Gertrude help?

Scenario 2, Internet – Based on a lesson idea found on the following page of the Poway (San Diego) High School web site: http://www.powayusd.com/PUSDPHS/--dbase/--dmoore/warquest/index.html

Elmo and Ricardo, two high school history teachers, were sitting in the library media center, planning their courses for the coming year.

"You know, Elmo, last year while the war was going on, it was a hot topic," said Ricardo, looking over the curriculum guide. "It seemed to spark the kids' interest in all kinds of related topics. Everyone wanted to know more about that region of the world and how our government works during a crisis; my students seemed even more interested in studying about past wars. But for kids this year, the whole thing will be old news again. This year, as we study the wars in which America has participated this past century, I'd like to try something new – something that would make a connection to their lives and bring home to them what wars mean to them personally."

"I know what you mean," said Elmo, nodding. "I saw a webquest the other day that I have been thinking we should try this year."

"What's a webquest?" asked Ricardo, looking up from his curriculum guide.

"Let me show you," said Elmo, going over to one of the center's computers. Ricardo followed him and sat down next to him as Elmo typed in the site URL.

"Webquests are online projects in which students solve a problem or create a product based on their research. In this webquest, each student takes a perspective on war from a list: nurse, statesman, poet, statistician, conscientious objector, war hero. We show them these questions: (1) Under what conditions would you serve your country to fight a war? (2) What types of conflict are worth a fight (war)? (3) What would you be willing to fight for? (4) When is war worth the costs of war? The best part is that the project web site helps schools like us pair up their students with students of their own age who live in a country that has experienced war. The partners communicate by e-mail and exchange information to answer the questions. The last activity is a joint letter they write to a person in government who has decision-making powers (i.e., President, congressperson, or a leader of another country), giving a summary of their findings about the costs of wars."

"This could be very powerful," said Ricardo, leaning back in his chair and putting his hands behind his head. "We could even have debates between groups of students. If we did videos of them, we could put those on the site, as well."

S2.1 What instructional problems did Elmo see that he felt a webquest could address?

S2.2 What would be the relative advantage of using a webquest format for this topic??

S2.3 What kinds of Phase IV planning tasks can you think of that would need to be done in preparation for this project?

S2.4 What outcomes would need to be assessed in this webquest, and how would you recommend they be assessed?

Problems to Analyze and Solve

P.1. Each year, Gill has his fifth-grade students identify an issue of current popular concern, e.g., local pollution problems, homeless or migrant people, quality of education for students with English as a second language. Gill has them use the Internet to research what other communities and groups are saying and doing about this problem. Then the students develop a position statement with a proposed solution and post it on the school's Internet. They request that feedback on their site be e-mailed to the teacher.

P1.1 What relative advantage does Gill see for using the Internet for this project as opposed to other resources?

P1.2 According to the textbook, what is the name for this kind of problem-based learning?

P1.3 Why do they have people e-mail feedback to the teacher rather than the students?

P.2. Larry is trying to get his English students to think about possible careers in journalism or other areas that require writing. He has his students contact one or more of the people he knows in these areas who have agreed to be interviewed online. They answer students' questions about how they entered the field, what they do on a daily basis, and what they do and don't like about their work. When they complete the interview, they write a summary and present it to the class.

P2.1 What relative advantage does Larry see for using the Internet for this project as opposed to other resources?

P2.2 According to the textbook, what is the name for this kind of online activity?

P2.3 Why doesn't Larry let the students research and find their own people to be their online information sources?

P.3. Each year, Prida has her ninth-grade students do a project in which they interview ninth-graders at other schools and create a newsletter documenting their current shared views and concerns and stories they feel are noteworthy. The newsletter is posted on the school's web page. When the newsletter is done, Prida contacts the teachers of the cooperating ninth-grade classrooms and gives them the URL for the newsletter. The teachers ask their students to create and e-mail Prida "Letters to the Editor" giving their comments and opinions about the newsletter stories.

P3.1 What relative advantages does Prida see for using the Internet for this project as opposed to other resources?

P3.2 What relative advantages do the other teachers see for having their students use the Internet and e-mail as opposed to other resources?

P3.3 What outcomes might Prida assess for this project and how would she assess them?

P.4. To introduce his unit on the American presidents, Lonnie has his students do a web-based scavenger hunt. He gives them a list of questions about Presidents and a list of web sites with annotations about the kinds of information they supply about the Presidents and other historical figures. He also has them document the search method they used to locate each of their answers. Then he asks them to write a brief description of other noteworthy facts/data they found in the course of the hunt. He awards several kinds of "prizes" for the hunt: most correct answers at end of allotted time, most efficient/organized search techniques, and best "other information" found.

P4.1 What relative advantages does Lonnie see for using the Internet for this project as opposed to other resources?

P4.2 Why do you think Lonnie recognizes three different aspects about the hunt?

P4.3 Do you think Lonnie should have his students work individually, in pairs, or in small groups to do this kind of activity? Explain why.

P.5. Each semester, Carla and Wally, science teachers in two different schools, give their students an ecological problem to solve related to conditions in their local area. After each class has collected data from online sources provided by Carla and Wally, they each have to analyze the data, figure out the cause of the problem, and create a proposed solution. They use the project web site to display their collected data and solutions. Local scientists and interested citizens are asked to judge the solutions and write an analysis of the feasibility of each. Then the students discuss their solutions and how they might improve them, based on the judges' input.

P5.1 What relative advantages do Carla and Wally see for using the Internet for this project as opposed to other resources?

P5.2 According to the textbook, what is the name for this kind of problem-based learning?

P5.3 Why would Carla and Wally have judges assess the answers, rather than evaluating the solutions themselves?

PART II REVIEW EXERCISES
Using the TIP Model to Integrate Technology Resources

Do **Exercises 1-4** on the Companion Website at: http://www.prenhall.com/roblyer. Click on the link for *Educational Technology in Action* Review Exercises, and use the links in each of the following sections to answer the review questions. Do **Exercise 5** by loading the Tutorials CD and using the file in the Part II Review Exercises Folder.

Exercise 1. Integrating Instructional Software

As you read in Chapter 4 of *Integrating Educational Technology into Teaching*, teachers choose and integrate instructional software (courseware) packages according to the functions they fulfill: drill and practice, tutorial, simulation, instructional game, and problem solving. The following are some good sources for high-quality software: Broderbund, Pearson Education Technologies, PLATO, Riverdeep Interactive Learning , Sunburst Communications, and Tom Snyder. Sources for Integrated Learning Systems (ILSs), which may include any of these software functions, include: Compass Learning, Pearson Interactive Technologies, and ScienceMedia eLearning Solutions.

II.1 The names and categories that companies give their packages do not always match the actual functions of the software. Using the companies listed above as sources of instructional software, select an example software title that fulfills each of the five functions. Describe how each might be used in a classroom lesson.

II.2 Most ILS's are now completely online, but some have other delivery options. Look at the ILS products offered by each company above; describe how each delivers its ILS.

Exercise 2. Integrating Software Tools

The International Society for Technology in Education (ISTE) has a variety of lesson plans for using various software tools, including those described in Chapter 5. Some of the software tools described in Chapter 6 of *Integrating Educational Technology into Teaching* are online. Also, see the puzzle-maker, lesson plan designer, test maker, and worksheet generator at the DiscoverySchool.com site.

II.3 Go to the ISTE site and do a search for each of the tools described in Chapter 5 (word processing or word-processing, spreadsheet, database). Select one lesson for each tool and describe how it integrates the tool into a classroom lesson.

II.4 Select one of the online software tools at the DiscoverySchool.com site and create a product that could be helpful in a classroom lesson.

Exercise 3. Integrating Multimedia/Hypermedia

When teachers use multimedia software for classroom projects or presentations, they often select *HyperStudio®* or *Microsoft PowerPoint®*. Macromedia's *Director® or Authorware®* are higher-end software packages for those who want to do more complex, full-featured designs. For video development software, teachers usually select *iMovie® or FinalCut Pro®* from Apple, Inc. or Windows Movie Maker® from Microsoft Higher-end programs include Adobe *Premiere®* and Pinnacle Edition® by Pinnacle Systems.

II.5   Imagine that you are a classroom teacher and want to have your students develop their own multimedia presentations. You want to write a proposal to a local company to fund the purchase of software for your classroom use. Since you have five Windows XP computers in your classroom, you want to purchase five copies of multimedia software. Check out the deals offered at the *HyperStudio®* and *Microsoft PowerPoint®*, then compare these prices with those at online "warehouse" stores such as PC Connection or Computer Discount Warehouse. Create a spreadsheet to compare the prices. Enter the company names in the spreadsheet as row names, and have two columns for the prices: Single Copy Price and License/Lab Pack Price.

II.6   Do this same activity for video development software.

Exercise 4. Integrating the Internet and Other Distance Resources

To prepare for Internet projects in which students create their own web pages, teachers need several materials. Among these are: web-page development software and assessment instruments to evaluate students' products. Netscape Composer® is free web page development software that is very simple for teachers and students to learn. More full-featured software includes Microsoft's FrontPage® and Macromedia's Dreamweaver®. For assessment tools, check out the rubrics on Kathy Schrock's Guide for Educators.

II.7   If you do not already have it on your computer, download the Netscape™ browser and create a simple web page. (For directions, see Chapter 11 in the booklet *Starting Out on the Internet* that comes with your textbook.) Compare its features with those of another software such as Microsoft's FrontPage® and Macromedia's Dreamweaver®.

II.8   Open your browser and go to the URL for Kathy Schrock's Guide for Educators http://school.discovery.com/schrockguide/assess.html). Bookmark it. Review each of the five rubrics for evaluating student's web page products. From the *Integrating Technology Across the CD* disc that came with your textbook, locate five lesson plans that call for students to create web page products. Tell which of the rubrics would be appropriate for assessing each product or if a new rubric would have to be developed.

   Exercise 5. Creating Classroom Products – Load the Tutorials CD that came with this book. Open the Adobe *Acrobat®* file for the *Netscape Composer®* tutorial, and create the product as the tutorial directs. (Adobe *Acrobat Reader®* is on the CD.)

Part III:
Using the TIP Model in the Content Areas

Chapter 11

Problem-based Exercises on Using the TIP Model to Integrate Technology into English/Language Arts and Foreign Language Education

---

Introduction to Technology in English and Language Arts Education

Literacy skills are so critical to success in school that there is a sense of urgency about students acquiring them soon enough and at a high enough level to be able to apply them to other learning tasks. However, teachers often find it difficult to motivate students to spend the necessary time on these skills. Technology integration strategies and resources that can help meet these challenges are described in detail in Chapter 10 of *Integrating Educational Technology into Teaching* (Roblyer, 2003) and are summarized briefly here:

- **Motivating students to write** – Students are notoriously reluctant writers, yet practicing writing is the only way they can learn to do it well. Strategies to encourage and support writing include: using story starter software; connecting students via e-mail or the Internet with other students at a distance; and publishing their individual or group writing products in desktop-published, multimedia, or web page format.
- **Making outlining easier and/or more visual** – Students can use outlining software to create planning outlines that are easier to revise than those developed in handwritten or typed form. Students who need a more visual connection between abstract ideas and written outlines find it helpful to do "visual outlines" with concept-mapping software.
- **Engaging students in editing and revising written products** – Word processing software has revolutionized writing instruction in the same way it has transformed office communications. Depending on how teachers use word processing in the context of their writing programs, students will write and revise more than they would in other formats. Word processing also has unique features (e.g., spelling and grammar checkers) that encourage students to improve mechanical aspects of their writing.
- **Motivating students to practice reading for comprehension and vocabulary development** – Since practice is also key to increasing reading comprehension and vocabulary, software packages may be used to make this practice faster and more fun. Interactive storybooks also help engage students in practicing these skills.
- **Making practice of reading, language skills, spelling, and grammar skills easier** – Word processing-based practice exercises or software-based practice exercises supply interaction and fast feedback to make it more likely students will practice these skills.
- **Engaging students in reading literature** – Finally, teachers use Internet sites and multimedia products to make literature come alive and engage student interest.

Introduction to Technology in Foreign Language Education

Foreign language instruction shares many of the same challenges as instruction for English as a first language, e.g., finding ways to engage students in reading and writing and motivating them to practice the language skills involved. The primary obstacle unique to second language learning is that teachers want students to speak, read, and/or write in a language other than English while immersed in an English-speaking culture. As with reading, writing, and literature skills in English, technology integration strategies and resources that can help meet the unique needs of foreign language learning are described in detail in Chapter 10 of *Integrating Educational Technology into Teaching* (Roblyer, 2003); they are summarized briefly here:

- **Motivating students to practice using the language** – Most current software designed to help students learn a foreign language is in a multimedia format. This allows students to hear the language spoken and even see videos of people speaking it in context. These packages have the same benefits as practice exercises for English: they supply interaction and fast feedback in an individualized, self-paced environment to motivate students to spend more time on the skills.
- **Virtual immersion into the culture of the language** – The greatest disadvantage for most students learning a foreign language is that they cannot travel to the locations where the language is in daily common use around them. They learn the language disconnected from the culture in which it is used, which makes the experience more abstract and, thus, more difficult to learn. Virtual field trips on the Internet and multimedia software provide a simulated immersion in the culture of the language.
- **Allowing connections and collaboration with other students for practice** – Working with other students who are using the language is another kind of immersion experience. Collaboration on webquests and designing web pages and multimedia products give students meaningful opportunities to use the language they are learning. E-mail projects can link students with native speakers of a language to help encourage practice and motivate students to do their best work communicating with the new language.

See English/language arts standards at: http://www.ncte.org/standards/
See standards for foreign language learning at: http://www.actfl.org/
(Click on Special projects.)

Problem-based exercises in this chapter give you hands-on practice in integrating technologies into English/language arts and foreign language instruction. Through scenario-based problem situations, you can see how teachers go about selecting and using these tools to support teaching and learning.

Scenarios to Read and Analyze – The following scenarios are examples of integrating technology-based strategies into curriculum lessons for English and foreign languages. After reading Chapter 10 in *Integrating Educational Technology into Teaching* (Roblyer, 2003), answer the questions about using the TIP Model to integrate these strategies:

Scenario 1, English instruction – Based on a lesson idea on the following page of the Tramline Field Trips web site: http://www.field-guides.com/lit/shake/

Dietrich, a history teacher at Bonhoffer High School, was at his classroom computer, his body shaking and tears streaming down his face, as his colleague Sabine, an English teacher, came by for their meeting. She did a doubletake as she looked in the door, then rushed in. "Dietrich, are you hurt?" she asked anxiously. Then she realized he was laughing.

"It's okay, Sabine," said Dietrich, wiping his eyes. "I was just looking at this Shakespeare site you told me we could use for our co-teaching project. This one page lets students create their own taunts in Elizabethan language. Look at the one I just did: 'Thou spleeny tardy-gaited pignut!' Isn't that great? I've been sitting here creating taunts."

"You scared me to death," said Sabine, smiling. "Yes, this is one of the reasons I thought it would be perfect. Did you see the page on this site about the bubonic plague and the one on Elizabethan dress? We could do several activities that combine my unit on sonnets with your European history unit. I thought we could use this 'taunts' activity and the other language pages to get them interested in the similarities and differences between the English spoken in Shakespeare's time and our own. Then we can move on to discussions of the events that helped shape Shakespeare's perspectives."

"Yes," Dietrich agreed, "This would really help set the stage, so to speak. I thought we might have them do a historical background scavenger hunt with some of the other history sites I've used for this period. Then we could have them do a *PowerPoint*® presentation of events that shaped the times in which Shakespeare lived."

Sabine said, "I'm hoping our students will find this and the other activities as interesting as you did. I have such trouble drawing comparisons between the 1600's and our own times, and helping them understand the language differences when they read Romeo and Juliet is so difficult. I hate to water it down just so they can understand the story." She pointed to a page on the site. "I thought I could use this sonnet page just before they write their own sonnets," she said. "It's so interactive, it really helps them get started."

"Yes" said Dietrich, "this will be one unit they'll tell their friends about."

S1.1 What problems did Sabine and Dietrich see that the Shakespeare site could help with? What are the relative advantages of the activities they are proposing?
S1.2 What would be some of the outcomes that they would want to assess?
S1.3 What kinds of assessment tools would they need to design to assess the outcomes?
S1.4 How might they handle two classes working together for this interdisciplinary unit?

Scenario 2, Foreign language learning – Based on a lesson idea found in: "Cyber Traveling Through the Loire Valley" by Jane Chenuau. *Learning and Leading with Technology,* 2000, Vol. 28, Number 2, pp. 22-27.

Madeleine the foreign languages resource teacher for the Paramount School District was having lunch with Claire, the Paramount Middle School's sixth-grade French teacher.

"So what are you planning this school year, Claire?" asked Madeleine as she scanned the café's menu. "I'll bet you didn't ask me here just to sample the crêpes du jour."

Claire smiled. "Yes, even though they are wonderful here. Madeleine, I'm so excited about my new project, I had to tell you about it. You know how I'm always trying to find ways to have my students translate things from English-to-French and back again? It's always a challenge to get them motivated enough to look up and learn new words they need to describe events and places in any depth. I always feel if I can find an activity they find compelling, they'll spend so much more time using the language and new vocabulary. I thought I'd begin with virtual field trips to the chateaux in the Loire Valley. Remember the trip I took there last summer? This is the next best thing to bringing them along with me."

Claire took a page from her book bag and showed it to Madeleine. "See this list of tasks? After I have them 'visit' the chateaux and learn about their histories, the students will work in pairs or trios to complete these tasks to design and draw their own chateaux. They place each one – virtually – somewhere in the Loire Valley. Then they use the French version of *AppleWorks*® to describe it and its history. We can scan their drawings to use on the web pages they will create. It's a cultural immersion activity, but for a clear purpose."

"I see what you have in mind," said Madeleine. "Each group's page can be put on the school's virtual showcase site. They'll love having their names on them! But will anyone besides you and they and few others be able to read all these pages written in French?"

"This is the best part," said Claire, pointing to the last task on the sheet. "They have a link on their page to the English translation which, of course, they have to do, too. So they have to do both kinds of translations. Then I link their pages to an introduction site, where I explain the project. Their names will be the links to each one. This project will cover three of the 'Five C's' in the Foreign Language Standards: Communications, Cultures, and Connections. However, I'll need more copies of the French *AppleWorks*® software so they can work either in my room or the lab. That will help them get everything done efficiently."

"We'd better talk about this over dessert," laughed Claire, signaling for the waiter. "Maybe some nice Napoleons will give us some ideas on how to conquer this problem."

S2.1 What instructional problems did Claire have that she felt this project could address?

S2.2 What is the relative advantage of this project compared to non-technology ones?

S2.3 What kind of assessment instrument was Claire showing Madeleine? How would you state the outcome(s) she is trying to assess with it?

S2.4 What other outcomes would need to be assessed and how could Claire assess them?

English/Language Arts/Foreign Language Integration Problems to Analyze and Solve

P.1. Mabel has noticed that her students do not prepare an outline to plan what they will write for a composition assignment. She has taught them how to do outlines, but they seem unwilling or unable to do them. They have a great deal of trouble organizing information in writing, and she thinks it might be better for them to create a diagram that shows in pictures how concepts are related. She has heard about a software tool that can help them do this activity easier and faster.

P1.1 What technology resource would help Mabel address this problem?
P1.2 What would be the relative advantage of using this resource as opposed to others?
P1.3 Would it be better to have the students work individually or in groups to do the activity? Explain why.

P.2. Gerald has his class work in small groups to create a short story. As a whole class, they discuss the plot and characters; then each group writes a part of the story. They exchange sections and critique each other's parts. Then they do a final version. After the draft is complete, they post the story on the school's web server along with stories posted from past classes.

P2.1 What would be the relative advantages for Gerald's students to use word processing for their drafts instead of doing typed or handwritten drafts?
P2.2 What would be the relative advantages of posting the story on the Internet when it is completed?
P2.3 What outcomes would Gerald probably want to assess in addition to quality of writing in the final product? Suggest a way to carry out this assessment.

P.3. Nate notices that some of his students make a lot of homonym/homophone errors in their writing. He decides to have them practice correct usage with a software package designed especially for this purpose. The software shows one sentence at a time with a word missing, and gives two possible word choices. Students pick one of the words, and the software tells them immediately if it is correct or not and why. Nate allows them to practice for no more than 10 minutes. As they end their session, the software tells them a total score and which words they still need to practice.

P3.1 What are the relative advantages to Nate himself to use drill and practice software to address this problem? What are the relative advantages to Nate's students?
3.2 Why does Nate allow them to practice for no more than 10 minutes?
P3.3 Would it be better for Nate's students to do the practice individually, in pairs, or in small groups? Explain why.

P.4. Sheila is helping her AP Spanish students prepare for the exam. Sheila knows that there will be a lot of vocabulary on the exam many of the students may not have encountered. She decided to offer them the opportunity to practice vocabulary using a Spanish drill-and-practice program she has available. However, she has only one copy.

P4.1 How would you recommend Sheila have her students use this one copy of the software?

P4.2 What would be the relative advantage of using this software?

P4.3 What data could Sheila gather to get some indication the program was helping her students be better prepared for the exam?

P.5. Jules would like to motivate his students to spend more time on their German translations. They will do practice exercises he creates for them only under duress. He hears about a web site that will link up individual students to an e-pal in a German school so they can communicate in both German and English.

P5.1 What would be the relative advantages for Jules to use this strategy with his students?

P5.2 How would you advise Jules to structure this project to make it most meaningful for both students in this country and in Germany?

P5.3 Would you advise Jules to encourage student to communicate with the German students from their home computers, if they have them? Why or why not?

Chapter 12

Problem-based Exercises on Using the TIP Model to Integrate Technology into Science and Mathematics Education

Introduction to Technology in Science and Mathematics Education

Mathematics and science share so much content and have such similar teaching challenges that it is logical they also share so many of the same technology integration strategies. No only do many science subjects require mathematics skills, but both science and math also have many abstract and/or complex concepts that students often find difficult to understand and/or master. Technology-based strategies can help teachers meet these and other challenges involved in teaching mathematics and science topics. These strategies and resources to carry them out are described in detail in Chapter 11 of *Integrating Educational Technology into Teaching* (Roblyer, 2003) and are summarized briefly here:

- **Helping students visualize abstract or complex concepts** – Mathematics is, by its nature, an abstract area. It is a language of symbols designed to help people communicate in a standard way about topics such as numerical relationships, measurement, and probability. Science, too, has many phenomena that cannot be observed directly but must be represented symbolically. Strategies that help make these abstract concepts more concrete for students just learning them include: software- and web-based simulations and manipulatives (e.g., *Geometer's Sketchpad®*), video-based scenarios to represent problems, and spreadsheet demos.
- **Supporting low-level calculations in high-level learning** – Although students are expected to learn basic math skills, many higher-level concepts in mathematics and science require many time-consuming basic calculations; doing them by hand is not only inefficient, it can interfere with learning. For these kinds of learning tasks, students use Calculators and calculator-based labs (CBL's), spreadsheets, and statistical analysis programs to do low-level calculations so they can concentrate on high-level concepts.
- **Facilitating data collection and analysis during experiments** – Experiments and hypothesis-testing often require time-consuming data collection and subsequent analysis of the collected data. Students can use handheld probeware (Microcomputer-based Labs or MBL's) to make data collection more efficient; handheld Calculator-based labs (CBL's) and statistical analysis programs help with the analyses. These are not only time-saving tools, but they are also the tools of modern science, so it is important that students see them in action and have opportunities to use them to solve problems.

71

- **Providing supportive inquiry environments** – Recent science standards emphasize the importance of inquiry skills, or being able to use a systematic, logical approach to identifying a problem and gathering information required to solve it. Environments that can support the learning of inquiry skills are so complex that they are difficult to create and manage. Web-based formats make these environments easier for teachers to set up and monitor, and their built-in feedback and support mechanisms make them easier for students to use as they learn inquiry skills.

- **Allowing communication and collaboration opportunities** – Electronic communications (e.g., e-mail and web pages) are becoming essential tools for scientists, so it makes sense that students would use them as they learn science skills. Students also find them useful for obtaining help from their teachers and other expert sources. Faster, easier communications makes it more feasible to have students working together on problems, which is both more motivating to students and a better reflection of problem solving in the workplace.

- **Helping students practice required skills** – Although de-emphasized in modern mathematics and science standards, students still have to memorize and call to mind quickly several kinds of facts and simple rules in both areas. Drill-and-practice and game software provide a fast, efficient way for students to practice and get immediate feedback on correctness. This strategy is especially important as students prepare for important timed tests. If the need is urgent, teachers can create their own drills using multimedia software or a test item bank.

See science standards at: http://www.nap.edu/books/0309053269/html/index

See mathematics standards at: http://standards.nctm.org/

Problem-based exercises in this chapter give you hands-on practice in integrating technologies into science and mathematics instruction. Through scenario-based problem situations, you can see how teachers go about selecting and using these tools to support teaching and learning.

Scenarios to Read and Analyze – The following scenarios are examples of integrating various technology-based strategies into curriculum lessons for science and mathematics. After reading Chapter 11 in *Integrating Educational Technology into Teaching* (Roblyer, 2003), answer the questions about using the TIP Model to integrate these strategies:

Scenario 1, Mathematics instruction – Based on a lesson idea found in: "Teaching Fractions using a Simulated Sharing Activity" by Joe Garofalo & Brian Sharp. *Learning and Leading with Technology,* 2003, Vol. 30, No. 7, pp. 36-41.

Elementary teachers Li and Alfred were talking after school in the teacher's lounge. "You look tired, Li," said Alfred. "Tough day?"

"Teaching fractions wears me out," sighed Li. "And I haven't even started it yet! I've been thinking for months about how I can do it better. It's not just keeping them interested in mathematics, although you know how hard *that* is! It's also that I just don't think they understand why they are learning things like division and fractions, you know?"

"I know exactly what you mean," said Alfred, sitting down at the table with a cup of coffee. "You want them to think mathematically and start seeing the connections. All they seem to want to do is get the problems out of the way as quickly as possible. I've tried various materials and strategies. Manipulatives seem to keep them interested longer, but I still don't think they get the significance of the concepts. Elle over at Topflight Elementary tried giving her students cookies and having them divide them up among various numbers of kids. What a disaster! They were intensely interested in the cookies, though."

Li sat up straight and looked at Alfred. "Cookies!" she exclaimed.

"Yes, that's right, she used cookies," said Alfred, sipping his coffee.

"No, it just reminded me of an online project someone at the district curriculum conference mentioned. It had kids sharing 'virtual cookies' with friends. They did the division with animations on a computer screen, but then they talked about *why* they chose the methods they used to divide them. I'll bet they could repeat each sharing session several times, if they wanted to. Why didn't I see this before? This could work! Sharing food is something they really identify with, and the online format makes it so much more feasible."

"It would be even better if the screen showed the fraction symbols as they did the division," said Alfred thoughtfully. "Do you know if it allows that?"

"I believe it does," said Li, "But I'm going to a computer right now and find out."

"Wait for me!" said Alfred. "I want to see how it compares with my own methods."

S1.1 What problems did Li see that the online format could help with?
S1.2 What are the relative advantages of doing this activity in a computer-based format?
S1.3 Would this activity be done best in an individual or small-group format? Explain.
S1.4 How could Alfred help Li compare the effectiveness of this strategy with others she had used? What outcome(s) could they use as criteria to compare results?

Scenario 2, Science and mathematics instruction – Based on a lesson idea found on the following page of the web site for NSF- and NASA-sponsored Project SkyMath at: http://www.unidata.ucar.edu/staff/blynds/Skymath.html#mod

Ingrid, the science teacher at Fastpace Junior High was sitting at her classroom computer when Claude, the math teacher dropped by to borrow a book.

"Hey, Ingrid, do you have that curriculum ideas text from the workshop?" he asked.

"Come on in, Claude," said Ingrid. "You might find this web site more interesting!"

"Find something good?" asked Claude, sitting down beside her.

"You know how we've been looking for a project that helps teach inquiry skills in a hands-on way and also helps students see how mathematics and science work together in the real world? Well, I think I just found it," said Ingrid, pointing to the screen.

"See," she continued, "it says here that the module has students learning mathematical principles by focusing on a single central concept from weather: temperature. It calls for students to work in small groups collecting and analyzing weather data. Then the site has them exchange data and messages electronically with students in other locations. They work together to identify and solve problems that have many possible solutions. Isn't this great?"

"How do they collect the data?" asked Claude. "Do they take actual readings or do they just look at data available on the Internet?"

"It looks like they do both," said Ingrid. "They learn how state, national, and world weather agencies collect data. Then they pose local weather-related questions, decide on a common set of data to answer them, and design a process for collecting the data."

"Sounds good for you," said Claude. "But how exactly does this relate to math skills?"

"Think about what they have to do with the weather data," said Ingrid. "For example, observing minimum and maximum temperatures, calculating average temperatures, and stating a 'typical temperature' in terms of a mode, median, and mean for a given data set. It also has them use weather data to identify and describe mathematically significant patterns in data sets and make predictions based on probabilities."

"Wow!" said Claude, "We could have them use a spreadsheet to graph pairs of Fahrenheit and Celsius temperatures and talk about slope and intercepts. Then we'd have them use slope of the line to develop the rule for converting Fahrenheit and Celsius scales. I can see how this could clarify some fairly abstract math concepts so well."

"All this and students working with classes in other locations. Wouldn't they love that?" said Ingrid. "Now if we can just arrange for your students to work with mine."

S2.1 What instructional problems did Ingrid see that this project could address?

S2.2 What would be the relative advantage of using technologies for such a project?

S2.3 What kinds of Phase IV planning tasks can you think of that would need to be done in preparation for this project?

S2.4 What electronic resources could help Ingrid's students work with Claude's?

Science and Mathematics Integration Problems to Analyze and Solve

P.1. Ariel, the AP mathematics teacher, wanted to have her students do simple correlations with two data sets to demonstrate the mathematical principles involved. However, it took students too long to do these calculations by hand and there were too many data entry errors using a calculator.

P1.1 What technology-based strategy could Ariel use to address this problem?
P1.2 What would be the relative advantage of using this strategy?
P1.3 Would it be better to carry out this strategy as a whole class or with students working individually or in groups? Explain how you would do it.

P.2. Boris was trying to show his teenage students in the business education program how they could figure out quickly how much car they could buy with the money they had. He wanted to show them the relationship between the down payment, interest rate, and length of the loan and how this all affected monthly payments and the total they would spend on the car at the end of the loan period. However, he wanted them to be able to do the calculations quickly, so they could focus on the underlying math concepts.

P2.1 What technology-based strategy could Boris use to address this problem?
P2.2 What would be the relative advantage of using this strategy?
P2.3 Describe the steps you might use to carry out a simple lesson using this strategy.

P.3. Ahmed wanted his students to take readings at a local stream to do an experiment on acid and alkaline substances in water. He wanted to use the handheld probeware devices when they went on the field trip. With these devices, they could collect the data, bring the readings back in a data file, and download the file to the computer for analysis. However, he had 27 students and only 15 handhelds.

P3.1 What grouping strategy could Ahmed use to make the available devices work well with this many students?
P3.2 Explain how you would advise Ahmed have his students carry out the strategy.
P3.3 What would be the relative advantage of using this strategy as opposed to manual methods of collecting the readings?

P.4. Lydia was the school counselor in charge of helping students prepare for the test her school district had developed to select those students eligible for the special math/science magnet program, which offered all expenses paid to those who were selected. She knew a lot about the kinds of items that would be on the test, and she knew some of the students needed to practice some of the skills.

P4.1 What technology-based strategy would you recommend Lydia use to address this problem?

P4.2 What would be the relative advantage of using this strategy, as opposed to a paper-pencil format?

P4.3 Should students practice individually, in pairs, or in small groups? Explain.

P.5. Guido's ninth-grade students had a lot of problems understanding many geometry concepts. They seemed to understand them better when he drew the figures and angles for them as he explained the concepts, but this was not feasible for every problem. It took too long, and he couldn't draw well enough to show everything clearly.

P5.1 What technology-based strategy would you recommend Guido use to address this problem?

P5.2 What would be the relative advantage of using this strategy?

P5.3 If Guido has 32 students in his class and only one computer, what would you recommend he do to carry out this strategy most effectively?

Chapter 13

Problem-based Exercises on Using the TIP Model to Integrate Technology into Social Studies Education

---

Introduction to Technology in Social Studies Education

Social studies is not one topic but many: civics, economics, geography, history, and political science, among others. The teacher's challenge is to show students that by studying these topics, they are really learning about themselves and their place in our society and our world community, that they are part of what President Bush in his 2001 Inaugural Address called "a long story – a story we continue, but whose end we will not see." Technology-based strategies can help teachers meet these challenges in teaching social studies topics. These strategies and resources to carry them out are described in detail in Chapter 12 of *Integrating Educational Technology into Teaching* (Roblyer, 2003) and are summarized briefly here:

- **Demonstrating more graphically the connections between students' lives and other times and cultures** – Recent events have shown how important it is for students to see more clearly the way in which our past shapes our present and that, although our culture is important, we are part of a world community of cultures. Strategies that help students make these connections include software- and web-based simulations, virtual field trips, and online projects with distant students.

- **Making geographic and mapping concepts more visual** – Students often find it difficult see the connection between the symbol systems we call maps and the real world around them. Software- and web-based mapping utilities can help students design and read maps more easily, and GIS and GPS systems help facilitate use of geographic and other data to research and explore connections among geography, population, weather, and other factors that contribute to our environment.

- **Engaging students in learning about history** – History is typically one the most difficult subjects to teach because the past is often so dry and unreal – and, therefore, uninteresting – to students. Technology-based strategies that can help make history come alive for students include: virtual field trips, software- and web-based simulations, and online and multimedia research and development projects.

- **Allowing communication and collaboration opportunities** – As with many other topics, students are often more motivated to learn about social studies topics when they collaborate with other students on research and development projects. E-mail and the Internet allow faster, easier communications to make this joint work more feasible.

- **Helping students visualize abstract or complex economics concepts** – Economics requires mathematic problem solving and presents many of the same learning problems as other mathematics topics. Using software- and web-based simulations lets students interact with systems in which economics principles are being used and can help make many abstract concepts more concrete. Also, students can do Internet-based research to obtain up-to-the-minute status information on financial conditions and see demonstrations that help clarify production and distribution principles.
- **Facilitating student practice in required skills** – As with mathematics and science topics, modern instruction in social studies does not emphasize memorization. However, there are still many facts students need to learn and memorize (e.g., states and capitals, countries in various continents). Drill and practice and instructional game software provide fast, efficient ways for students to practice and get immediate feedback on correctness as they learn these facts.

See social studies standards at: http://www.ncss.org/standards/

Problem-based exercises in this chapter give you hands-on practice in integrating technologies into social studies instruction. Through scenario-based problem situations, you can see how teachers go about selecting and using these tools to support teaching and learning.

Scenarios to Read and Analyze – The following scenarios are examples of integrating various technology-based strategies into curriculum lessons for social studies. After reading Chapter 12 in *Integrating Educational Technology into Teaching* (Roblyer, 2003), answer the questions about using the TIP Model to integrate these strategies:

Scenario 1, Social studies instruction – Based on a lesson idea found in: "At the Source" by Terry Hongell and Patty Taverna. *Learning and Leading with Technology*, 2003, Vol. 30, No. 6, pp. 46-49.

Nick, an elementary school teacher, was sitting in the school computer lab when Margaret, the school principal, came in. "There you are, Nick," said Margaret. "I've been looking all over for you. I wanted to see if we could place another student in your class."

Nick sighed. "Sure, Margaret, why not? If I can find a way to interest the ones I've got, one more should be no problem."

"You sound a little perplexed, Nickie," said Margaret. "Anything I can do?"

"Maybe you can listen to me talk through this. Did you ever try to create one project that met a bunch of different criteria?" asked Nick. Margaret nodded and sat down. "Well," continued Nick, "I want to get my fourth graders interested in studying local history, but I want it to be something they can all identify with. I'd like them to do some research on it, but not just copying down stuff from an encyclopedia. I want them to do it in a way that gets them thinking about *how* to do research, and how they should synthesize information after they find it. I want them to work in groups, so they can learn how to collaborate and cooperate; even at their age, I think it's so important they have opportunities to do this. Finally, I want them to create something that we can display; you know, something tangible that reflects their work and what they learned – something they can show their parents."

"You never do anything simple, do you, Todd?" laughed Margaret. "Get any ideas yet?"

"Maybe I have," said Nick. "We could study a local hero from our own town: Colonel Cresap. Everything around here, including the school, is named after him, and I know there would be a lot on the Internet about him. The kids could work in groups, each one using web sites to research an aspect of his life. I could create a little booklet for each group to keep track of its work and to put in text and images we could add to a project web site."

"You could ask his great-great-granddaughter, Doreeda Cresap Downs to come and speak to the class. I'll bet she'd have some great photos you could scan," said Margaret.

"That's right," said Nick. "We could video her and put it on the site. We could even include a visual timeline with the images. Give me 50 more students; I'll handle 'em all!"

S1.1 What problems did Nick see that the online project could help with?
S1.2 What are the relative advantages of doing this activity in this format?
S1.3 What should Nick include in his booklet to help students synthesize information?
S1.4 What outcomes should Nick assess and what methods could he used to assess them?

Scenario 2, Social studies instruction – Based on a lesson idea from the Tramline Field Trips web site: http://www.tramline.com/tours/cross/world/_tourlaunch1.htm

Virginia, a high school history teacher, walked into the Band Room just as Carter, the school's band director, was finishing a summer workshop with a group of flute students. "Hi, Carter, everything humming along here?" she said brightly.

"You and your music puns," said Carter, gathering up sheet music. "You're probably here about the benefit concert, but I can't talk now. I'm meeting with parents about the proposed band trip. We've been asked to march in a parade in London, you know."

"Yes," said Virginia, "Actually, that's why I wanted to talk to you. Some of the other teachers and I have come up with a way to merge the trip with our social studies curriculum and, at the same time, give students who can't go on the trip a chance to participate in it."

"How would that work?" asked Carter. "I feel bad about so many students not being able to afford to travel that far. It would be wonderful if everyone could go."

"In a way, they can," said Virginia. "The trip won't be until December. What we'd like to do this coming semester is plan a different activity that relates to the trip for each of several classes. There is an Internet site called 'Windows on the World' that we could use to guide the activities. It has everything you should know about international travel. There is a section on passports and other legal aspects of preparing to travel abroad, one on changing currency, another on time zones and, of course, there are several U. S. State Department sites that give travel warnings and describe how an embassy works in a foreign country. We could use the *CIA World Factbook* site to research information about England and France – I know you all will want to take the Chunnel over to Paris before you come home. The site even has an interactive World Map and, of course, we can use *Mapquest®* to prepare an itinerary and follow you as you go. LuAnn would like her science class to track the weather as you travel to various locations and use the Travel Health section of the Centers for Disease Control site. We could prepare our own web site to display our findings.

"But best of all," she continued, "I think we can give a few students digital cameras and handheld computers to take with them. They can take images and video and keep a journal to send back the same day to us as we follow your trip. We could put it all on our band trip web site and update it daily as you guys travel. It will be like the whole school is going with you. What do you think?"

"Ginny, I think you've come up with an award-winning arrangement!" said Carter.

"Carter! A music pun!" laughed Virginia. "On that note, I guess I'll go start planning."

S2.1 What problems did Virginia see that this project could address?
S2.2 What would be the relative advantage of using these technologies for the activities?
S2.3 What kinds of Phase IV planning tasks can you think of that would need to be done in preparation for this project?
S2.4 What would Virginia have to do before placing these images on the school web site?

Social Studies Integration Problems to Analyze and Solve

P.1. Dale wanted to show his sociology students how they could test hypotheses about correlations among social factors such as population centers and crime statistics. He had heard of a technology tool that would allow students to do this with maps, so they could see at a glance if their hypotheses were correct.

P1.1 What technology-based strategy could Dale use to address this need?
P1.2 What would be the relative advantage of using this strategy?
P1.3 What would you suggest Dale have his students produce to show the results of their work? How might he assess this product?

P.2. Francesca's students would be studying the Early American period in our country's history in the Spring semester, and she wanted to make the class more engaging than it had been in the past. She wished she could have her students visit places like Williamsburg, Philadelphia, and Monticello, but they did not live near any of these sites.

P2.1 What technology-based strategy could Francesca use to address this problem?
P2.2 What would be the relative advantage of using this strategy?
P2.3 What could Francesca's students produce to show what they had learned? How might she assess this product?

P.3. Alison's social studies students were about to study the U. S. Constitution. She not only wanted to show them what was included in our Constitution, but she also wanted them to see all the factors that must be considered when any new country creates a charter to guide its development and reflect its national principles. She had heard about software that allowed students to do this in a role-playing way.

P3.1 What technology-based tool could Alison use to address this need?
P3.2 What would be the relative advantage of using this strategy instead of holding a class discussion on this topic?
P3.3 Should students work individually, in pairs, in small groups, or as a whole class on this activity? Explain.

P.4. Fern wanted to have her students study about their local area, so she arranged to have them work via e-mail with a class of students in another state. They exchanged background information about each other's locations and asked questions about weather conditions, favorite spots to visit, and other items of interest to both. Finally, they each worked on a travel brochure that included a local map and summarized the information they had gathered. They ended the project by e-mailing each other a copy of the brochure.

P4.1 What problems did Fern address with this technology-based strategy?

P4.2 What would be the relative advantage of using this strategy, as opposed to having students do a brochure without contacting other students?

P4.3 What outcomes should be assessed in such a project, and how might they be assessed?

P.5. Levar's students were studying how the stock market both reflects our country's economy and helps shape it. He asked them to track five stocks over the course of two months and chart their progress. At the same time, they tracked events in the country and the world that may affect stock market performance for the stocks they picked. They ended the project by describing the events that corresponded with major dips and peaks and how they think these events affected the stocks.

P5.1 What problems is Levar addressing with this technology-based strategy?

P5.2 If Levar had the students work in small groups on this activity, explain how this strategy might best be carried out in the classroom.

P5.3 What would be a good way for Levar to have students present their findings? Explain why this presentation strategy would be effective.

Chapter 14

Problem-based Exercises on Using the TIP Model to Integrate Technology into Art and Music Education

---

Introduction to Technology in Music Education

Although it strikes some people as incongruous that machines could transform an area that emphasizes personal creativity, computers and other electronic devices have done just that in the music curriculum. Technology has been thoroughly integrated throughout the spectrum of music instruction, from composition to skills practice. Technology's role in music education is unique in that it supports so many teaching techniques that would not otherwise be feasible in a typical classroom. Technology-based strategies to support the teaching of music are described in detail in Chapter 13 of *Integrating Educational Technology into Teaching* (Roblyer, 2003) and summarized briefly here:

- **Allowing easier creation and editing of individual and group music composition** – Students come to understand music best when they create it. Without technology, writing and editing notation for student-created musical pieces would be a laborious and tedious process. Musical instrument digital interface (MIDI) keyboards, in combination with sequencers and music editors, make it easier for students to play their own musical pieces, see the musical notations that result from them, change the music notations quickly and easily, and combine their work with that of other students.
- **Making possible monitored practice** – With systems that connect a teacher station to keyboards and students with headphones, it is also easy for teachers to monitor and assist individuals as whole classrooms of students play at the same time.
- **Supporting individual performance practice** – Sequencing programs also make it possible for teachers to supply an entire orchestra, minus the tracks of one or more instruments, so students can practice a given piece by themselves and *en ensemble*.
- **Providing easy access to musical selections** – In music appreciation, Internet sites and multimedia collections make it easier for teachers and students to access quickly and easily information about composers' backgrounds and hear samples of their works.
- **Facilitating student practice in required skills** – Practice is a way of life for musicians, and technology can make it more likely that students will spend the time they need on practice. In addition to the support technology provides for performance practice described above, drill-and-practice and instructional game software provide a fast, efficient, motivational way for students to do skills practice such as identifying keys in which music is written and names of notes on a scale.

Introduction to Technology in Art Education

- **Fostering creativity through production and manipulation of images** – With digital equipment and image manipulation software, students can build their creative skills as they develop and store their original images or change existing ones.
- **Making possible novel graphic design techniques** – Many graphic techniques (e.g., tweening, morphing) can be done only with computer software. Software tools let students explore graphic design in unique ways.
- **Allowing easy sharing of creative works** – By digitizing creative works and placing them on disk or web sites, students can more easily share their work with others and allow teachers to review them and offer critiques.
- **Providing easy access to images of artworks** – Technology can support art appreciation in the same ways it does music appreciation. Internet sites and multimedia collections make it easier for teachers and students to access quickly and easily information about artists' backgrounds and view samples of their works. Virtual field trips and scavenger hunts are ways to motivate students to look at the available sites.

See music standards at: http://www.menc.org/publication/books/standards.htm

See art education standards at: http://www.ed.gov/pubs/ArtsStandards.html

Problem-based exercises in this chapter give you hands-on practice in integrating technologies into music and art instruction. Through scenario-based problem situations, you can see how teachers go about selecting and using these tools to support teaching and learning.

Scenarios to Read and Analyze – The following scenarios are examples of integrating various technology-based strategies into curriculum lessons for music and art. After reading Chapter 13 in *Integrating Educational Technology into Teaching* (Roblyer, 2003), answer the questions about using the TIP Model to integrate these strategies:

Scenario 1, Music – Based on an idea in: "Music Technology in an Inner City Intermediate School" by Shelley Jacobson, 1993. *The Computing Teacher*, Vol. 20, No. 8, pp. 33-34.

Willa, music director for the elementary school, was talking with Henry, the school district music coordinator, after a professional development workshop. "I know it will take some doing. I plan to have two fund-raising activities this year alone, both with the help of some of the more music-minded parents, but I think it will be worth it. By next year, I plan to have an entire MIDI network in the music room."

Henry frowned, "Is that the best use of your resources, Willa?" he asked. "Think how many instruments and how much sheet music you could buy with what it will take to set it all up. Remember you'll need to get music editing software, and keyboards, as well."

"Yes, that's all in my plan," said Willa, patting her notebook. "In my visits to some of the larger districts up north, I've seen some wonderful things happening when teachers use these resources. They told me that students who had never had an interest in music caught the bug when they were able to create their own songs; and when kids saw the notation come up when they played a tune on a keyboard, you could just see the light snap on in their heads! They got so excited about embellishing their tunes and, of course, it was so easy with the music stored in the system. They could just bring it up again anytime."

"But will it be worth all the money and time it will take you to set it up?" Henry asked incredulously. "Think of the maintenance! What will happen when something breaks?"

"Henry, I'll be able to teach 30 kids at one time in one room – all playing a different version of 'Heart and Soul!'" said Willa, laughing. "With sequencers, we'll even be able to let more advanced students play in ensemble pieces with different parts. I'm so excited!"

"Well, it will make it easier for our kids to practice their basic music skills," said Henry. "I've seen the merits of the practice software you bought last year. But the costs ..."

"Wish me luck, Henry!" said Willa, walking quickly toward towards the group of administrators in the front of the room. "I'm going to catch the superintendent before she leaves. She has a daughter in fourth grade; maybe we can get a little help with funding."

S1.1   What problems did Willa see that the MIDI network could help with?
S1.2   What are the relative advantages of having it, as opposed to the music resources Henry described?
S1.3   What data should Willa collect to show Henry the technology resources are making a difference in students' learning and are worth the investment of time and funds?
S1.4   What planning tasks should Willa do to address some of the items Henry brought up?

Scenario 2, Art – Based on a lesson idea in: "From All Sides Now: Weaving Technology and Multiple Intelligences into Science and Art" by Carol Lach, Ellen Little, and Deborah Nazzaro. *Learning and Leading with Technology,* 2003, Vol. 30, No. 6, pp. 32-35, 59.

Chauncey, a fourth-grade teacher, and Etienne, art resource teacher, were on a field trip with students to a local museum of natural history. "This is a great opportunity for the kids," said Chauncey, as he looked over a display of shells. "Thanks for agreeing to help out."

"Hey, no problem," said Etienne good-naturedly. "I've been wanting to talk to you anyway about an idea I've had for a project that combines art and science."

"Really?" said Chauncey. "Sounds kind of neat. What do you have in mind?"

"Well," said Etienne. "It occurred to me when I observed your class last year that you are teaching a lot of concepts about how things are structured in nature, you know, repetitive patterns found in shells, flowers, and so on. I liked the way you described how nature works in patterns, that it's predictable."

"Thanks," said Chauncey. "I'm not sure how many of the kids really get it, though. Sometimes I can just see their little eyes glaze over when we talk about permutations."

"I know what you mean," said Etienne. "But how about if we made it a little more interactive and had them do something to make the concept a little more concrete for them? We could give them a collection of some objects like leaves and plants we have gathered. For some objects, we could give them digital pictures. We also give them a group of patterns and structures and ask them to look for them in the objects. I envision them working in small groups – maybe divide up the collection among the groups, you know? Then when they have matched up the patterns with the objects, we have them create a tree or flower or shell of their own on the computer by drawing and repeating the pattern they found and moving the copies around. They could even paint the patterns different colors on-screen. Then we could print out the products and display them. I've seen projects like this done, and the kids sometimes come up with some really beautiful pieces."

"I don't think this lesson would take very long to do," continued Etienne. "Maybe an hour or so for each of two days. Would that fit in with your science periods?"

"I think it would be great," said Chauncey, looking at Etienne with astonishment. "What a creative idea, Etienne! I guess that's why you're the artist, huh?"

"Ha! It's much more challenging to get the kids to be artists!" said Etienne, smiling. "Or better yet, getting them to see the art in science and vice versa. Maybe this will help."

S2.1 What problems did Etienne feel this project could address?

S2.2 What would be the relative advantage of using image software for the activities?

S2.3 What would be some additional ways to display students' work in addition to printing it out and posting it?

S2.4 What data should Etienne and Chauncey collect to see the impact of this lesson on students' learning and attitudes?

Art and Music Integration Problems to Analyze and Solve

P.1. Orson, a music performance teacher, has been talking to his friend and colleague Liam, who is a music teacher in Dublin, Ireland. Orson and Liam would like to have their students work together on creating new musical pieces based on a series of Irish folk tunes that Liam has collected in the rural areas near the city. Liam would send recordings of the tunes, and the students would play them and work on variations based on them. However, the teachers and students need a way to make both the music production tasks and communicating their products faster and easier.

P1.1 What technology-based strategies could Orson and Liam use to address these needs?

P1.2 What would be the relative advantages of using these strategies?

P1.3 What would be a good way to display their products, once they were created?

P.2. Danielle, the school's music teacher, is doing an interdisciplinary project with Merrill, the history teacher. They plan to have Merrill's students research backgrounds of the musical composers of the Romantic period, listen to some of their works, and locate information on events of the times that helped shape their perspectives and, consequently, the music they created.

P2.1 What technology-based strategy could Danielle and Merrill use to carry out such a project?

P2.2 What would be the relative advantage of using this strategy?

P2.3 If they wanted to have Merrill's students work in small groups, how would they implement this in Merrill's class?

P.3. Students in Hadley's music appreciation class were preparing for their end-of-semester recitals. There were a variety of musical pieces, and Hadley would be accompanying each student during the recital. He wanted students to be able to practice individually with accompaniment, but he did not have time to accompany each of them as they practiced.

P3.1 What technology-based tool could Hadley use to address this need?

P3.2 What would be the relative advantage of using this strategy instead of allowing them to practice without accompaniment?

P3.3 If Hadley has 30 music students and only 8 stations, what strategy could he use to allow each student to practice individually?

P.4. Lucien wanted to teach his art students some visual literacy skills he had been reading about. He had heard that these skills were becoming increasingly important for students as consumers of news information and potential buyers of products. He wanted to show them how easy it was to create fictional images that looked real or alter real images to create false impressions.

P4.1 What technology-based strategy could Lucien use to address this need?
P4.2 Why could this skill probably not be taught in a non-technology way?
P4.3 How could Lucien arrange this activity so students could work on it in groups?

P.5. Samantha was an art resource teacher in a small, rural school district. She wanted her students to have opportunities to look at and appreciate various works of art and learn something about the artists. However, they were far from any art museum, and there was no money for field trips even if there was one close by.

P5.1 What technology-based strategy could Samantha use to address this need?
P5.2 What planning would Samantha have to do before she introduced this activity to students?
P5.3 What could Samantha do to help structure this activity to keep students on task?

Chapter 15

Problem-based Exercises on Using the TIP Model to Integrate Technology into Health Education and Physical Education

Introduction to Technology in Health Education

The more we find out through research and experience about what it takes for people to lead longer, healthier lives, the more important it becomes to help them learn and begin to apply this information to their own lives at an early age. However, health-related issues are interrelated with students' attitudes and beliefs and are frequently difficult to influence through school instruction. The visual, interactive nature of video and multimedia technologies can play a uniquely powerful role in raising students' awareness of important health information and changing their perspectives on health and fitness. Technology-based strategies to support the teaching of health concepts are described in detail in Chapter 14 of *Integrating Educational Technology into Teaching* (Roblyer, 2003) and summarized briefly here:

- **Clarifying human physical functions** – For many young people, the body is a mysterious and unknown territory. Their lack of knowledge about how it works can result in assumptions that could prove dangerous. Software- and web-based simulations allow students to explore this territory in a very visual way, making unseen, internal processes observable and easier to understand.
- **Helping students visualize and monitor characteristics of healthy lifestyles** – Students need models of healthy behavior to help them see the behaviors they need to adopt. Video-based demonstrations and simulations can provide these models, and web-supported projects give students opportunities to practice and tools to help monitor desirable behaviors.
- **Assisting with presentations of controversial issues** – Modern society is filled with controversial issues students need to know about and shape their own opinions on. Many teachers have difficulty talking to students about these issues, and students can be uncomfortable listening to adults discuss them. Video presentations and software- and web-based simulations offer safe, private environments for learning sensitive topics.
- **Helping students obtain accurate, reliable information about health issues** – As students learn about health issues and start to ask their own questions about healthy and unhealthy behaviors, they need objective, reliable sources of information. Carefully selected Internet sites can be an invaluable source of knowledge and insights on diseases, treatments, prescription and over-the-counter drugs, and human problems such as addiction and domestic violence.

Introduction to Technology in Physical Education

- **Demonstrating and providing feedback on physical performance** – In sports and other areas of physical performance, students need models of what they are aiming for, as well as errors to avoid. Videos and software- and web-based simulations can provide models that can be viewed whenever and as many times as students need to see them.
- **Helping students monitor fitness and performance indicators** – As students begin to set goals for personal fitness, they need quick and easy ways to monitor their progress toward their goals. Handheld computers and electronic monitoring devices (e.g., heart monitors) can help supply this vital information; software such as spreadsheets and specially-designed software can help them store their information so they can compare their performances across time.
- **Supporting interdisciplinary approaches** – As both health and physical education become optional, rather than required, courses in school curriculum, it becomes increasingly important to integrate activities that emphasize health and fitness concepts into instruction for other disciplines. Group-based Internet and multimedia projects help provide a way to accomplish this.

See health standards at:

http://www.aacps.org/AACPS/BOE/INSTR/CURR/health/nhestandard.htm

See physical education standards at:

http://www.aahperd.org/naspe/template.cfm?template=programs-ncate.html#standards

Problem-based exercises in this chapter give you hands-on practice in integrating technologies into health and physical education. Through scenario-based problem situations, you can see how teachers go about selecting and using these tools to support teaching and learning.

Scenarios to Read and Analyze – The following scenarios are examples of integrating technology-based strategies into curriculum lessons for health and physical education. After reading Chapter 14 in *Integrating Educational Technology into Teaching* (Roblyer, 2003), answer the questions about using the TIP Model to integrate these strategies:

Scenario 1, Health – Based on the "Nutrition Track" lesson from the *Microsoft Productivity in the Classroom* collection. ©1997 by the Microsoft Corporation.

Ophelia, the science resource teacher for the school district, was talking with Fred, a science teacher from the middle school. "I wonder if I could interest you in trying a curriculum project I heard about at the regional conference last week?" asked Ophelia.

"Sure," said Fred. "I've enjoyed working with that human body simulation program you told me about last year. The kids get a kick out of seeing those processes work and naming the parts of their body in each system."

"I think they'll like this, too," said Ophelia. "You know how I'm always looking for ways to show students 'healthy ideas' they can apply to their own lives. I saw one on nutrition that I think would be great."

"It better have fireworks in it," said Fred, laughing. "Their mothers harangue them so much about eating right, they don't want to hear it anymore."

"This is a good one, I think," said Ophelia. "It's very hands-on, which I know is a criterion for all your science projects, and it makes the idea of a healthy diet a more visual concept for them. I think it will get them engaged in monitoring their own diets."

"Let's hear it," said Fred. "I'm engaged in it already."

"Good!" said Ophelia. "You begin by looking on the U.S. Department of Agriculture's web site. They have the Food Pyramid there and a recommendation for what you should eat on a daily basis to maintain a healthy diet. Then you give them a page to track what they eat for five days. They can calculate their average results and create pie charts showing the average number of servings for each food group in their diets. This lets them see clearly how their diet compares, on average, to the USDA's recommended diet."

"That's a lot of calculating," said Fred. "And they have a hard time drawing pie charts."

"You use a spreadsheet to keep the data," said Ophelia. "It draws them automatically."

"This sounds great," said Fred. "After all the weight I gained over the holiday, maybe I should track what I eat along with them. I could use a better approach to my own nutrition."

S1.1   What problems did Ophelia see that this project could help address?

S1.2   What are the relative advantages of using technologies to support this approach, as opposed to having students do the data-keeping and summary charts by hand?

S1.3   Describe an efficient arrangement for students to enter their data and do calculations.

S1.4   How could Ophelia get an indication of whether or not this project changed student attitudes about their eating habits and maintaining better nutrition?

Scenario 2, Physical education – Based on a lesson idea from the Kids 'n Fitness web site at: http://exchange.co-nect.net/Teleprojects/project/?pid=16&cid=3

Roberto and Marina, physical education teachers from the same school, were talking after a basketball game. "That was fun," said Roberto. "It's good to see so many of the students here. However, sometimes I think watching a game is as close as many of them will get to real physical fitness."

"Yes," sighed Marina, "Now that physical education courses are no longer required at our schools in this district, it's getting more difficult for them to stay in shape; the results are noticeable. Everyone expects kids will do an after-school sport, but it doesn't always happen that way. I think even the principal has lost sight of how the lack of physical exercise affects students and, ultimately, can have an impact on their work in school."

"That's right," agreed Roberto. "That's why I wanted to talk to you about an online project I found out about the other day at a meeting."

"A computer project?" said Marina, "That's all we need is for them to spend even more time indoors on electronic gadgets."

Roberto laughed, "No they don't sit at a computer to do this activity, but I'll bet they will want to check the project site once in awhile to see our school results."

Marina looked at Roberto doubtfully. "Let me explain," said Roberto. "There is a web site where schools around the country submit how much they've exercised in various kinds of activities. Teachers can sign up their classes to submit their results and compete with other schools. I've talked to Wilber, the math teacher, and he's agreed to let me introduce the project in his classes. We show students a series of exercise activities they can do, and Wilber has agreed to create a spreadsheet to keep track of the exercises they submit. He'll award points to students each week they turn in an exercise summary. At the end of each week, he'll use the spreadsheet data to build a graph of their performance and post it outside his class in the hall. Then he'll submit their data to the web site, and they can see how they compare. We thought we'd tell the principal about the project, too, so he'll have our results read on the morning announcements. I'll be he'll encourage the kids to exercise so we can compare favorably with other schools! What do you think?"

"I think it's inspired!" exclaimed Marina. "Who would have thought computers can motivate students to exercise more?"

S2.1 What problems did Roberto feel students have that he felt this project could address?

S2.2 What would be the relative advantage of using image software for the activities?

S2.3 What would be a good way to arrange for students to be involved with putting the data into the spreadsheet and checking the web site?

S2.4 What data should Roberto collect to see the impact of this project on students' exercise patterns after the project ends?

Health and Physical Education Integration Problems to Analyze and Solve

P.1. Felicia wanted all her physical education students to keep a "fitness portfolio." She wants them to enter weekly entries on what they have accomplished on their own fitness plans and on assigned exercises and activities, their entries on a fitness journal, and video clips of their performances. She wants them to be able to update it and share it easily with other students and their parents and friends.

P1.1 What technology-based strategies could Felicia use to address these needs?
P1.2 What would be the relative advantages of using these strategies?
P1.3 Why does Felicia want students be able to share the portfolio easily with parents and friends?

P.2. Whenever his tennis students are practicing various new skills he has just introduced, Larue takes videos of their performances with his digital camera. Later that day, he and the students look at their performances together and analyze how they could improve their techniques.

P2.1 What problem(s) does this technology-based strategy address?
P2.2 What is the relative advantage of using this strategy?
P2.3 What are two reasons Larue may want to use a digital video camera as opposed to a regular video camera to record students' performances?

P.3. Estelle wants her students to be prepared for drug-related situations they may encounter outside school. She knows that it does no good to talk to them about what they should do in these situations. She has found a software package that includes a set of short videos, each with a different drug-related scenario. At the end of each scenario, students have an opportunity to choose from a list of responses and see what might happen after each choice.

P3.1 What problem(s) does this technology-based strategy address?
P3.2 What is the relative advantage of using this strategy?
P3.3 Should students work individually, in pairs, in small groups, or as a whole class on this activity? Explain.

P.4. Corey knows that his 10th- and 11th-grade students have and will have a lot of questions about issues related to drugs, sex, and domestic violence. They will be graduating soon, and he wants to make sure they know some of the places they can go for accurate, reliable information from health agencies and other authoritative sources. He decides to have them do an in-class scavenger hunt to locate answers to various questions by looking at some of the key sites.

P4.1 What problem(s) does Corey's technology-based strategy address?

P4.2 What is the relative advantage of using this strategy as opposed to just giving them a list of the web sites?

P4.3 Should students work individually, in pairs, in small groups, or as a whole class on this activity? Explain.

P.5. Elise is a physical education teacher who wants each of her students to set fitness goals for themselves. She has students decide how many exercises of each kind they will do each week and what their target heart rate should be. She has them keep track of how well they have met their goals. However, keeping this information in the notebook she has set up for each class is becoming cumbersome and difficult to update. In addition, she cannot easily calculate averages across the class or how much a student has fallen short of or exceeded a goal.

P5.1 What technology-based strategy could Elise use to address this need?

P5.2 What would be a good way to organize the ongoing task of entering and updating student information? Should Elise do it or should the students? Explain.

P5.3 What could Samantha do to help structure this activity to keep students on task?

Chapter 16

Problem-based Exercises on Using the TIP Model to Integrate Technology into Special Education

---

Introduction to Technology in Special Education

Special education, like social studies, is not one area, but many. However, it is unique among the disciplines, since it is delineated by student characteristics, rather than by content. Students in special education range from those with unusually high talents to those with severe mental and physical disabilities. Technology resources have been used successfully in all these areas, but have had especially dramatic results with students who have deficits. Technology-based strategies to support instruction for all special education areas are described in detail in Chapter 15 of *Integrating Educational Technology into Teaching* (Roblyer, 2003) and summarized briefly here:

- **Compensating for students' physical deficits to allow full participation** – Devices and software are available to allow students who could not do so otherwise to receive information or complete class assignments. For students who cannot use regular keyboards for computer input, there are alternate keyboards and/or word completion or word selection software. Students who cannot speak intelligibly can do so by using "talking" (speech synthesized) word processing software or software that lets them select words from a computer screen and produce speech-synthesized responses. Students with visual deficits can use text enlargement software, software that reads to them, and/or machines that produce their work from Braille input. Students with hearing deficits can use software that presents information in text form or through close-captioned video.

- **Allowing collaboration in mainstreamed classes** – Many of the technology resources that help support small-group work (e.g., multimedia and web page development projects) also require tasks at many different levels of difficulty. This kind of learning environment allows students to work together despite varying ability levels.

- **Allowing multiple ways to demonstrate learning** – Online research and multimedia/web page development projects allow gifted students opportunities to use their various talents. Those who are good at writing or structuring information can work cooperatively with those who excel at music or graphic design; each can make a valuable contribution to the product; each learns valuable skills in working with others.

- **Supporting students' organization and study skills** – Students with mental and physical disabilities often have difficulty processing and organizing new information. Interactive study tools and personal organizers help motivate students to work on these important skills.

- **Skills practice** – Although not recommended as the sole or even primary use of technology for students with mental disabilities, drill-and-practice and instructional game software frequently can provide the private, high-feedback environment that can encourage these students to learn basic skills.

See standards for special education teachers at:
http://www.nbpts.org/standards/stdsoverviews.cfm
(Look under "Exceptional Needs")

Problem-based exercises in this chapter give you hands-on practice in integrating technologies into special education. Through scenario-based problem situations, you can see how teachers go about selecting and using these tools to support teaching and learning.

Scenarios to Read and Analyze – The following scenarios are examples of integrating various technology-based strategies into curriculum lessons for special education. After reading Chapter 15 in *Integrating Educational Technology into Teaching* (Roblyer, 2003), answer the questions about using the TIP Model to integrate these strategies:

Scenario 1, Special needs – Based on an idea in "Multimedia and Students with Learning Disabilities: The Road to Success" by Michael Speziale and Lynne LaFrance, 1992. *The Computing Teacher*, Vol. 20, No. 3, pp. 31-34.

Rob, the vocational English teacher, was designing a web page on his classroom computer when Jessica, the mother of one of his students, dropped by.

"Hey, Rob, see any good sites?" said Jessica, looking over his shoulder.

"Hi, Jessica!" said Rob. "Yes, as a matter of fact, I just had a great idea for a curriculum project, and I'm designing a web site to support it. I hope it'll be a good one."

"Is this another activity Eric can do?" asked Jessica. "You seem to have a way of making him feel like he is an important part of your class; he loves coming here."

"I'm glad to hear that," said Rob amiably. "Yes, this is another one I'm hoping Eric will find very interesting. He is probably one of my young teenagers hoping to get a driver's license, right? Well, I thought I would have my class create an online study guide of the state driver's manual. It will give them lots of practice in reading and writing, and they'll learn a lot about structuring information for others to read."

"Doing this online guide, it sounds difficult," said Jessica. "With all Eric's reading disabilities, will he be able to do the work?"

"Yes, I've thought about that," said Rob. "You know several of my students have reading difficulties; two of them have already failed the written portion of the driver's exam and are really discouraged. I'm going to pair each of them with a student who reads comparatively well. Then we'll divide up the driver's manual and have each pair work on a section. They'll summarize the rules and use pictures to clarify them. I thought we'd scan in images from the manual, and they can create others as they feel they need to have them. Then, we'll put each section on a web page, and I'll create the main page to link with all the sections. I thought we'd finish by having each pair create a little quiz over the material in their section and add that to the site. Then we could have the students try to answer the questions in class. Of course, they can use this guide to study whenever they need to."

"I think this will be another one Eric will love." said Jessica. "Wait until I tell him!"

S1.1   What problems did Rob see that this project could help address?
S1.2   What are the relative advantages of using online technologies to support this approach, as opposed to having students prepare a guide in paper format?
S1.3   How could Rob arrange to have all the student pairs working at the same time?
S1.4   On what kinds of outcomes should students be assessed?

Scenario 2, Special needs – Based on an idea in "Practical Ideas: Literature, Computers, and Students with Special Needs" by Diane Schipper. *The Computing Teacher*, Vol. 19, No. 2, pp. 33-37.

Irving, a language arts teacher in the middle school, helped his student Mali begin her work at the computer. As she began to use the Braille-enhanced keyboard to type her story, the speech synthesizer read her words aloud. Irving showed Mali how she could turn off the voice whenever she wanted to, then turn it back on to read passages she had written.

As the system continued reading the passages aloud, teachers who were walking by peered in the door to see what Irving was doing. Nadine, the Spanish teacher, could not contain her curiosity and walked in. "Irving, what is this? A reading robot?" she asked.

"Nope, just a talking word processor, Nadine" said Irving. "Mali here has problems seeing the screen, and this helps her keep track of what she is writing, doesn't it, Mali?"

The girl nodded and smiled. "Yes, this is great!" she said. "Now I'll be able to write so much faster and get more done. When I hear it read to me, I can spot what I am doing wrong so quickly."

"I'm also thinking of using this software with David, my student with speech difficulties," said Irving. "This will let him type his communications to us, and we can understand what he says better. I'm thinking it may also help him with his written language development. You know, he has problems with his writing, as well as speaking."

"You don't think he will be put off by the speech-synthesized voice, do you?" asked Nadine.

"I don't think so," said Irving. "Mali likes it, and the other kids seem intrigued by it."

"I wonder if it could help my students with reading disabilities," said Nadine. "Perhaps if I pair them with students who are better readers and they work together on a written product, the speech synthesis could give the poorer readers auditory feedback on what they write. What do you think, Irving?" she asked.

"I think it's worth a try," said Irving. "We should do whatever we can to help these guys use language better – even if it means using 'reading robots,' right?"

S2.1 What problems did Irving have that using this system could address?

S2.2 What would be the relative advantage of using this system with Mali? With David?

S2.3 When other students are present, what could Irving do prevent them from being disturbed by the talking computer as Mali uses it?

S2.4 What would be a good way to find out if David dislikes the speech-synthesized voice and if he and/or Nadine's students produce more and/or better-written work as a result of the software and synthesizer?

Special Education Integration Problems to Analyze and Solve

P.1. Cordelia had a student with cerebral palsy who could not control her hands enough to write or use a computer keyboard. Cordelia believed her student was bright; she contributed some valuable things verbally and seemed interested in everything they did. However, she was unable to complete most class assignments.

P1.1 What technology-based strategies could Cordelia use to address these needs?
P1.2 What would be the relative advantages of using these strategies?
P1.3 Should Cordelia have her student with cerebral palsy work alone or with other students? Explain.

P.2. Arturo was a science teacher who had been assigned to teach a group of gifted students. The principal had asked Arturo to create learning activities that would challenge and motivate these students to learn science and mathematics and offer a way they each could demonstrate individual learning using particular kinds of intelligence.

P2.1 What technology-based strategy could Arturo use to carry out such a project?
P2.2 What would be the relative advantage of using this strategy?
P2.3 Describe how Arturo might manage this kind of activity in a classroom.

P.3. Bart was a fifth-grade teacher who had three low-achieving students with very low mathematics test scores. It was clear they each lacked basic skills in math facts and operations. Bart had no time to work with each of these students individually, but he knew they needed practice in the skills they lacked. They also needed motivation to practice the skills, since each had failed so frequently in previous classes.

P3.1 What technology-based strategy could Bart use to address this need?
P3.2 What would be the relative advantage of using this strategy?
P3.3 Should these students work individually, in pairs, or as a small group on this activity? Explain.

P.4. Theodore was a seventh-grade social studies teacher who had two students with learning disabilities. Neither student could read or write very well. However, both had talents. One was an avid photographer, and the other liked to draw and paint. Theodore wanted to create an activity that allowed them to participate fully in classroom projects and have their talents recognized. He felt this recognition would help motivate them to spend time on other learning activities.

P4.1 What technology-based strategy could Theodore use to address this need?

P4.2 What would be the relative advantage of using this strategy?

P4.3 How could Theodore determine whether or not these two students felt more positive about other class work as a result of participation in this activity?

P.5. Zeke was a fifth-grade teacher. He had a nonverbal student whose vocal cords had become injured in a traffic accident. The student was very intelligent, but he was depressed and discouraged because he could not communicate with his teachers or his classmates. Zeke had overheard some of the children referring to this student as "The Dummy." Zeke wanted to find a way to allow this student to communicate in class to show the other students he was not a "dummy" and allow him to participate more fully in learning activities.

P5.1 What technology-based tool could Zeke use to address this need?

P5.2 What would be the relative advantage of using this tool?

P5.3 Give an example of a learning activity in a content area (e.g., language arts, science, social studies) that would make use of this tool.

PART III REVIEW EXERCISES
Using the TIP Model in the Content Areas

Do **Exercises 1-6** on the Companion Website at: http://www.prenhall.com/roblyer. Click on the link for *Educational Technology in Action* Review Exercises, and use the links in each of the following sections to answer the review questions. Do **Exercise 7** by loading the Tutorials CD and using the file in the Part III Review Exercises Folder.

Exercise 1. Integrating Technology into Language Instruction

Technology-based strategies can help achieve standards for <u>English/Language Arts</u> and <u>Foreign Languages</u>. In the *Integrating Technology Across the Curriculum* disc that came with your textbook, do a search on lesson ideas in each area; read some of the examples.

III.1   Review the six integration strategies for English/language arts listed in Chapter 11, page 65 of this booklet. Create a lesson idea based on one of the six strategies. Tell which of the <u>English/Language Arts Standards</u> your lesson could help meet.

III.2   Review the three integration strategies for foreign languages in Chapter 11, page 66 of this booklet. Create a lesson idea based on one of these strategies. Tell which standards under the five "C's" for <u>Foreign Languages</u> this lesson could help meet.

Exercise 2. Integrating Technology into Math and Science Instruction

Technology-based strategies can help achieve the standards for <u>mathematics</u> and <u>science</u>. In the *Integrating Technology Across the Curriculum* disc that came with your textbook, do a search on lesson ideas in each area; read some of the examples.

III.3   Review the three technology integration strategies for mathematics listed in Chapter 12, page 71 of this booklet. Create a lesson idea based on one of these strategies. Tell which of the <u>mathematics standards</u> this lesson could help meet.

III.4   Review the three technology integration strategies for science listed in Chapter 12, page 72 of this booklet. Create a lesson idea based on one of these strategies. Tell which of the <u>science standards</u> this lesson could help meet.

Exercise 3. Integrating Technology into Social Studies Instruction

Technology-based strategies can help achieve the standards for <u>social studies</u>. In the *Integrating Technology Across the Curriculum* disc that came with your textbook, do a search on lesson ideas for this area; read some of the examples.

III.5   Review the six technology integration strategies for social studies listed in Chapter 13, page 77-78 of this booklet. Create a lesson idea based on one of these strategies. Tell which of the <u>social studies standards</u> this lesson could help meet.

Exercise 4. Integrating Technology into Music and Art Instruction

Technology-based strategies can help achieve the standards for <u>music</u> and <u>art</u>. In the *Integrating Technology Across the Curriculum* disc that came with your textbook, do a search on lesson ideas in each area; read some of the examples.

III.6   Review the five technology integration strategies for music listed in Chapter 14, page 83 of this booklet. Create a lesson idea based on one of these strategies. Tell which of the <u>music standards</u> this lesson could help meet.

III.7   Review the four technology integration strategies for art listed in Chapter 14, page 84 of this booklet. Create a lesson idea based on one of these strategies. Tell which of the <u>art standards</u> this lesson could help meet.

Exercise 5. Integrating Technology into Health and Physical Education

Technology-based strategies can help achieve the standards for <u>physical education</u> and <u>health</u>. In the *Integrating Technology Across the Curriculum* disc that came with your textbook, do a search on lesson ideas in each area; read some of the examples.

III.8   Review the four technology integration strategies for physical education listed in Chapter 15, page 89 of this booklet. Create a lesson idea based on one of these strategies. Tell which <u>physical education standards</u> this lesson could help meet.

III.9   Review the three technology integration strategies for health listed in Chapter 15, page 90 of this booklet. Create a lesson idea based on one of these strategies. Tell which of the <u>health standards</u> this lesson could help meet.

Exercise 6. Integrating Technology into Special Education

In the *Integrating Technology Across the Curriculum* disc that came with your textbook, do a search on lesson ideas for special education; read some of the examples.

III.10 Review the five technology integration strategies for special education listed in Chapter 16, page 95-96 of this booklet. Create a lesson idea for students with disabilities based on one of these strategies.

III.10 Create a lesson idea for gifted students based on one of these strategies

 Exercise 7. Creating Classroom Products – Load the Tutorials CD that came with this book. Open the Adobe *Acrobat*® file for the Microsoft *Excel* tutorial, and create the product as the tutorial directs. (Adobe's *Acrobat Reader*® is on the CD.)